Involvement Bulletin Boards
and Other
Motivational Reading Activities

M. Ellen Jay

Linnet Books • 1976 

Library of Congress Cataloging in Publication Data

Jay, M   Ellen.
     Involvement bulletin boards and other motivational
reading activities.

     Bibliography: p.
     1. Bulletin Boards. 2. Reading—Audio-visual aids.
I. Title.
LB1045.J38 1976b   372.4'14   76-25190
ISBN 0-208-01617-1

First published 1976 in a paperbound edition
as a Gaylord Professional Publication by
Gaylord Bros., Syracuse, N. Y.

and

as a Linnet Book by
The Shoe String Press, Inc.
Hamden, Connecticut

Printed in the United States of America

Contents

Preface

There is need for beauty in everyone's life, and in many schools bulletin boards are used to provide visual joy. However, bulletin boards can offer educational experience as well as beauty. Indeed, when students have the opportunity to participate in solving riddles and puzzles or searching for answers, they tend to pay more attention to the board than they do merely when walking past it.

Bulletin board construction is time consuming, but if it becomes an educational activity as well as a decorative or amusing one, the time is put to good use. It is from this rationale that the concept of involvement bulletin boards was developed in our school, and there is evidence that the students both enjoy and learn from this approach.

Believing that others will want to try involvement bulletin boards of their own, this book is designed to provide ideas to help interested teachers get started both in classrooms and in media centers.

In preparing this book I have had the enthusiastic help of the teachers and pupils of the elementary schools in the Montgomery County, Maryland, System. Also, I have enjoyed the invaluable assistance of Dr. Hilda L. Jay, Media Specialist of the Ridgefield High School, Ridgefield, Connecticut, my mother, who long before this book has been a great model and encourager.

Illustrative material for *Involvement Bulletin Boards* has been created or adapted by the author, who also took the photographs.

M. E. J.

I

Initiating an Involvement Program

Planning

As a result of cooperative planning between media center personnel and classroom teachers, involvement bulletin boards located in the area of the media center can be tied in with classroom activity in such a way that these boards become additional learning stations for the classroom teacher to use. Small groups of students may be sent by the classroom teacher to the media center to engage in the activity for a specified length of time.

The media center specialist may plan the current board to use some search skill being promoted in the media center, while at the same time the activity incorporates content related to classroom program. An example of this double thrust is the board combining questions about the circus with the use of sub-headings in encyclopedia articles (p. 28). A further example is the bulletin board combining seasonal interest in snow with skill in identifying the key word for use in the encyclopedia index (p. 24). Specific example 4 in *Snow* asks if children during the Civil War had coasting sleds. Students soon found that looking up *sleds* left the question partially answered. A further search was required to identify the dates of the Civil War to compare with the date given for the introduction of coasting sleds.

A broad topic such as biography, fiction by theme, or an author's works can be used to promote reading at a variety of levels. For example, the Beatrix Potter board (p. 38) asks for picture identification of characters in part 1 which is an activity any age student can accomplish. Part 2, the puzzle based on a single story, requires additional reading skills, and Part 3, the biographic questions, requires critical reading skills. A popular board can attract large numbers of students. It is an advantage to plan boards so that students may begin work with any section of the board.

Another aspect of cooperative planning is the time element. A board, to be useful to the classroom teacher, must be up long enough to allow for student participation. An involvement bulletin board activity will be most suitable for one grade level; however, experience has shown that it will be used by several grades. Therefore, before taking a board down, it is advisable to check with the teachers as some of them may be planning to use it "next week." If it is a single classroom that has continuing interest in the board, it can be taken down and reassembled in that classroom.

Specific outcomes may have been designed by the planners, but individual teachers often adjust the requirements for completion to better suit their students' needs. An example of this is related to the board on the National Parks Centennial celebration (p. 73). The original intention was to require the students to identify the park name. However, the fourth grade teachers who were studying United States geography, required their students to identify the state in which a national park is located as well as identifying the park.

If answer sheets are to be used, cooperative planning is advisable to determine in advance who will do the correcting for the students.

Location of Involvement
Bulletin Boards

The corridor bulletin board nearest the media center is usually the best choice since this location allows equal access for all students. Being adjacent to the reserve shelves is helpful when problems posed by the involvement bulletin board activity require student research. Furthermore, this location allows for supervision to be shared by media center personnel and classroom teachers, fostering a closer relationship between classroom and media center programs.

Boards within the media center or a specific classroom can also be used effectively. Variety is important. The same board does not always have to be the involvement activity one, and not every display needs to be of the involvement type.

Techniques

Opaque projector.—The opaque projector, used as an enlarger, transforms almost anyone into an artist. The smallest sketch may be made as large as desired (although it might take a two or three step process to produce a very large size). The directions for using an opaque projector in this manner appear in numerous audio-visual textbooks and guides (See the bibliography). Sometimes older students or aides enjoy doing this part of the process for the teacher.

Lettering.—Individual letters cut from colored construction paper, wrapping paper, or fabric scraps; or those drawn on a strip of paper freehand or with the aid of large stencils, or those commercially made pin-back plastic or ceramic letters can be used effectively for captions. One should keep in mind that younger students can not read cursive writing; therefore, if they are to be involved, manuscript must be used for captions and directions. Also, problems do arise when pin-back letters are placed within the reach of students. Who can resist rearranging these letters? Basic principles of freehand lettering and of cutting block letters from paper are available in arts and crafts books.

Another need for lettering is that used on direction sheets and question cards. These are effectively done using a primary typewriter.

Color.—Color serves a variety of purposes. It draws attention, unifies the total board, provides symbolic meanings. In addition, if the planner uses color as a code to relate various parts of the activity, it facilitates student use of the board. For example, when doing a crossword puzzle, mount the clues on the same color construction paper as the ink used to label (number) the answer boxes, such as red for down and green for across.

Directions.—A copy of the directions needed to complete the activity should be posted as part of the involvement bulletin board. These directions should be specific, in sequential order, and clearly worded. In this way, students gain competence in reading and following printed directions. The clearer the directions, the less assistance the students will require to complete the activity.

Layout.—Artistic layout principles are available in numerous guides (See bibliography); however, there are additional considerations regarding placement or size of the materials used on the board. The ability level of one's students determines the number of questions to be used, which in turn determines the size of the print used and the ultimate size of the pieces to be displayed.

More students can work simultaneously when they can begin work at various points. One way to accomplish this is to design an involvement bulletin board that incorporates a variety of activities. These activities can be of varying difficulty and thereby can provide for individual differences. Examples of this technique are found in the Beatrix Potter board (p. 38), the Weather board (p. 88), and the State Shapes board (p. 75).

Answer sheets.—Answer sheets should be designed for simple correction. If the questions are worded properly, the student will have to apply higher level thought processes to arrive at the answer, but the notation of the answer need not be complicated. An example of this is the number code used on the answer sheet for Hidden Word Puzzles (p. 34).

Crossword puzzles.—Crossword puzzles require special thought. In creating your own puzzles, first decide whether the puzzle will be based on a single story, an author's works, or a reading list. Next, make a list of relevant words to be used as answers. Manipulate these words until the format of the puzzle is achieved. It is not essential that every word on the original list be incorporated into the puzzle. Finally, write the clues the students will use. It has been found helpful to place a small directional arrow indicating down or across in addition to the numbering of answer boxes. Use of a two-color system further aids the student in working the puzzle; e.g., red clues and numbers for down, and green clues and numbers for across. Whenever possible, avoid using answer words when writing clues.

Prizes.—Prizes should not be used as a regular reward. However, students do receive motivation from seeing their names added to a list of those students who have completed a puzzle or from receiving a duplicated certificate prepared for every student who completes a special involvement bulletin board activity. Perhaps once a year a small prize (such as the bite-sized candy bar used with Seasonal Dictionary Game: Hallowe'en (p. 19) is useful. The problem with prizes is that the concept of working for fun and personal challenge can be overshadowed by the desire to acquire the prize. Any time prizes are used, everyone completing the activity should receive the same reward.

Lamination.—Especially successful and potentially reusable figures and question cards should be preserved for future re-use. This can be accomplished by using plastic fixitive sprays, clear contact, or, if you have access to the required supplies and equipment, laminating them. Do not plan to reuse materials annually. However, after a lapse of at least three years, materials appear new to most students, and it is possible to use the entire board or parts of it in a new format.

Intellectual Growth

The students' intellectual growth proceeds by perfecting processes and by acquiring fact. Involvement bulletin boards provide opportunity to follow directions, build vocabulary, learn to categorize, improve search skills, gain proficiency in reading, develop critical thinking, improve independent work habits, as well as acquire facts. All of this is accomplished in a pleasant game-like way.

The subject matter or theme of the involvement bulletin board can be taken from any curricular area. National holidays, seasonal interests, and special events can also be used. On occasion, the content of an involvement bulletin board does not capture the students' interest and the activity is ignored by them. Don't give up; the next one will catch student interest and opportunity for intellectual growth will resume. Before judging a board unsuccessful, be sure you have allowed sufficient time for it to catch on—especially the first ones you try. Once students have experienced fun from involvement bulletin board activity, they watch for additional ones. However, a number of students will tend to hang back until a friend or student leader is observed enjoying the activity before doing it themselves. This is similar to a student's being encouraged to read a book when he observes a respected name already on the book card. A seasonal involvement bulletin board will probably be up about three weeks. Others may need as much as six weeks to serve all students interested in doing the activity.

Teacher's Responsibility
for Encouraging Student Use

If involvement activities are to be used to their fullest, then it must be realized that responsibility must be shared by classroom teachers and media center staff. When the two work together, the students have much to gain.

The initial joint planning of activities is excellent, but it is not enough. The classroom teacher must be genuinely interested in the program. Teachers need to include the activities as a part of required classroom work, and this means allowing time in their classroom day for students to be able to participate.

Participation can be a required part of daily work. It can be done for extra credit. It can be a reward for work completed. It can provide a change of atmosphere for under-achieving students. It can be used to reduce class size when work in the classroom with a smaller group is necessary or desirable.

Classroom teachers need to consider all types of student skills, and to recognize that although the content of an involvement activity might not directly correlate with on-going unit content, the skills being used and developed through participation in the activity are skills that need to be practiced repeatedly.

Going out from a classroom in a traditionally constructed school might be more appealing to students than moving about in an open space school where movement is much more common. However, it should be remembered that involvement activity centers can be located anywhere in the building to facilitate their use as a teaching tool.

Maintaining an Idea File

The teacher who becomes convinced of the value of involvement bulletin boards to the students' program should start an idea file for reference. A card file provides a handy means for noting the location of a particular diagram or illustration in a book, or the words of a potentially useful quotation read in a non-standard source. Clippings from newspapers and advertisements can be attached to a card and placed in this file, especially if 5 x 8 cards are used. Whenever possible the original source should be cited on the involvement bulletin board; therefore, this information should be noted on the file cards.

Remember that it is the *idea* that is being saved for adaptation. The size of the original layout is not important. Small sketches can be enlarged, and large ones can be cited on a file card and stored elsewhere. Some of the large ones come from commercial store displays. When possible, it is a good idea to establish a contact who is in a position to save these items for you when they have served their original purpose and are ready to be discarded.

Some types of placemats used in restaurants are another source of ideas and information.

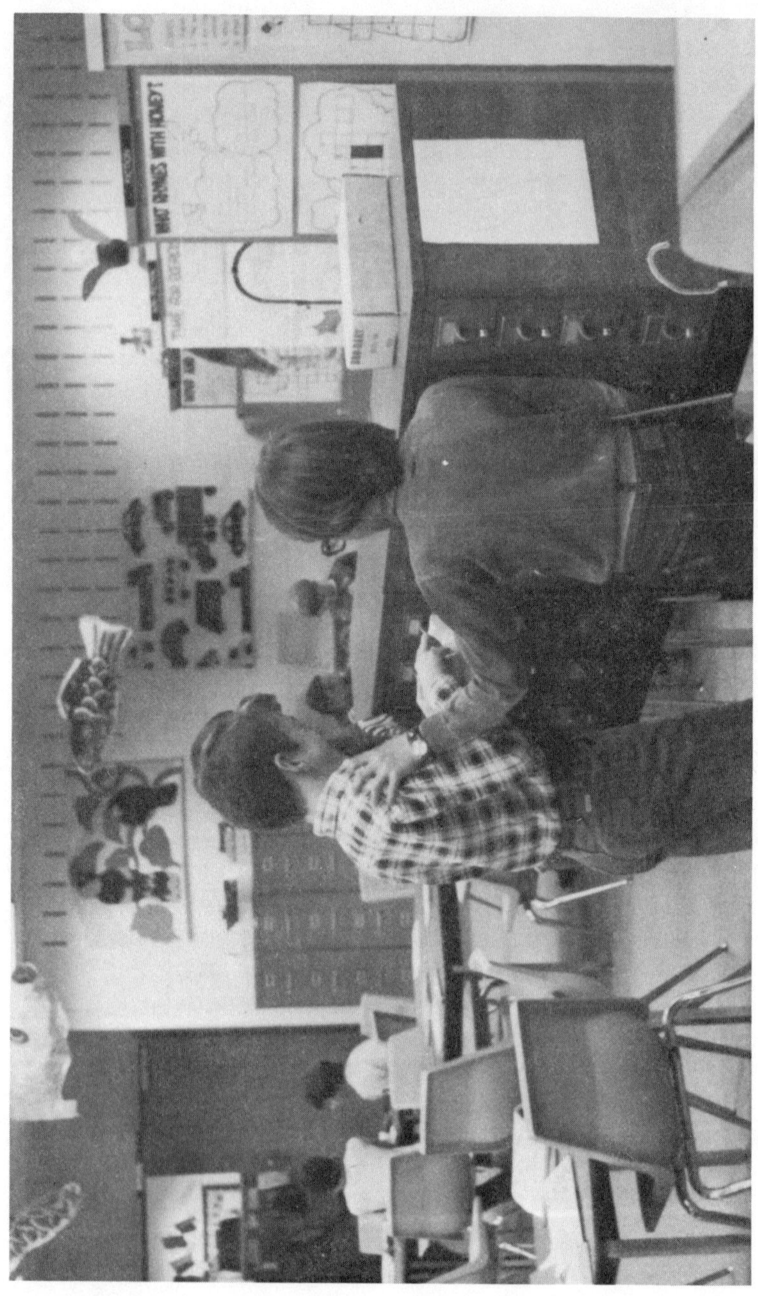

II
Ideas for Involvement Activities

LIST OF ACTIVITIES

Seasonal Dictionary Game

Materials

List of words (Thesaurus is a good tool.)
Unabridged dictionary
3 x 5 cards
Primary typewriter, or felt-tip pens
Colored construction paper for letters for caption
Seasonal pictures

Procedures

Create the word list which is based on a seasonal theme.
Type or print one word on each card.
Display these cards in the vicinity of the dictionary.
Use seasonal pictures to attract attention.

Student Behaviors

Student copies words onto his paper leaving space for
    definitions.
Student looks up the various words and discovers the shades
    of meanings for words with similar meanings.
Student writes down the meanings.
Student takes completed answer sheet to be checked.

Specific Examples

1. Our theme was Hallowe'en. The caption read "If you can
    define these tricky words, I will give you a treat!" (A bag of
    bite-sized candy bars was used for the "treat.")

2. The words used were: ghost, banshee, boggart, fiend,
genie, gnome, ghoul, goblin, hag, harpie, phantom,
shade, shadow, specter, spirit, spook, troll, witch, wizard.

Unexpected Outcomes

The activity was planned for older students, but some younger ones became interested. Students are selective
about their "treat" choices; not everyone likes chocolate.
Caution: To keep from having to replace treat supply,
limit their use to actual winners and keep them out of
sight of snacking teachers.
The activity is easily adapted for any holiday or season.

Christmas Traditions Around the World

Materials

Construction paper—several sheets green and scraps of
assorted colors
4x6 index cards
Reference materials about Christmas customs
Primary typewriter
Transparent tape

Procedures

Read through reference materials and devise questions.
The number of questions should match the number of school
days remaining until the holiday.

Make a large Christmas tree from the green construction
   paper.
Make a Christmas tree "ball" for each question. Cut a circle
   from an index card and one of matching size from colored
   construction paper.
Type or print the question on the card circle.
Hinge the colored circle to the card using transparent tape
   in such a way that the "ball" can be opened for reading.
The questions are to be answered one each day, somewhat
   in the manner of opening windows on an Advent calen-
   dar. Place the opening day's date on the cover of "balls."

Student Behaviors

The student lifts the colored cover of a "ball," reads the question, and searches for the answer.

Answers are written on pieces of paper and turned in to the librarian for checking.

Specific Examples

Questions are of two types. Some concern traditions and others concern Christmas stories.

1. In what country do they celebrate Christmas with a Piñata? What is a Piñata?
2. When and where was the first Christmas card printed?
3. Why do Canadians feed their cats extra well on December 24?
4. What would you eat for Christmas dinner if you lived in Finland?
5. In Italy who comes down the chimney with gifts? On what day does this happen?
6. Who were the first people to use decorations on Christmas trees?
7. What little words can you make using the letters in the word CHRISTMAS?
8. Where do French children put their shoes on Christmas Eve?
9. What is the day after Christmas called in England?
10. In what book does Santa go around taking the beards away from the false Santas?
11. *Mince Pie And Mistletoe* is a collection of Christmas _______ .
12. In what book was the story of how *Silent Night* was written told by a mouse?
13. In what book does a mouse get a name and a little red suit?
14. In what book do you meet Davy, who by freeing a fox from a trap learns how the animals celebrate Christmas?
15. What title did Santa give Rudolph for his help in guiding the sleigh?

Unexpected Outcomes

The idea of a question a day was ignored. Students would
start with the designated question, but could not stop
with one. They sometimes completed all the questions in
one or two days.
A caption was added which read: _____ Reading Days Until
Christmas. The number was changed daily.

The Twelve Days of Christmas

Materials

Large-sized illustrations of the Twelve Days of Christmas
made from book or greeting card illustrations, or original student art work
Construction paper strips

Procedures

Post illustrations (after enlarging and coloring, if necessary).
Create questions of a counting nature.
Post questions near illustrations.

Student Behaviors

Students use illustrations to calculate answers to the questions.
Answers will be checked by the media staff.

Specific Examples

Questions may be similar to the following:
1. What is the total number of people?
2. What is the total number of birds?
3. What is the total number of kinds of food?
4. What is the total number of musicians?
5. What is the total number of legs?

Unexpected Outcomes

After helping numerous students, a shortcut to the mathematical operations became evident: two times the sum of the people plus bird legs equals the total number of legs.

Is a French Hen food? A Partridge? A Turtle Dove? Be sure you have made your own determinations before launching this project.

Do You "Snow" the Answer?

Materials

Construction paper—both white and assorted colors
5 x 8 cards
Primary typewriter
Felt-tip pens

Procedures

Read through available reference materials and devise questions to be typed or printed on cards.

Cut a few large snowflakes from white paper.

Enlarge or sketch pictures relevant to the questions. Items such as an igloo, iceberg, sled, ice skates, skis, and snowshoes will attract the students' attention. Cut letters for the caption and post it.

Student Behaviors

The students read the questions and use available reference materials to find the answers. They write out the answers and hand them in for checking.

Specific Examples

These questions were suggested by the articles in *Worldbook*, and they were directed to third and fourth grade students.

1. The record for the biggest snowfall for a 24 hour period was set in what year, in what city, and how much snow fell?
2. Snow storms usually occur after what?
3. No two snowflakes are just alike, but all snowflakes have the same number of sides. How many sides does a snowflake have?
4. Did children during the Civil War have coasting sleds? When did they come into use in the United States?
5. What is the best type of snow plow to use to clear deep drifts? How does it work?
6. What is a snowdrop?
7. What were the first skis made of? What are modern skis made of?
8. What is the important characteristic of each of the three types of ice skates?
9. Is an iceberg made of fresh or salt water? Is there more iceberg showing above the water or hiding below?
10. What is an ice breaker? What is the name of the biggest one?
11. What is sometimes used as a window in an igloo?
12. Why does wearing snowshoes keep you from sinking into deep snow as you walk?

Unexpected Outcomes

The attempted humor in the title was above many students.
They constantly pointed out that the word "know" was
misspelled.
The key-word concept was important in this activity.

Find the Animal Word

Materials

Ranger Rick magazine, February, 1974
Construction paper—red and white
Felt pen—black
Opaque projector
Primary typewriter
Sheet of plain paper

Procedures

Enlarge the drawings from the magazine using red and white
construction paper and a black felt-tip pen.
Write the additional phrases on strips of construction paper.
Create the caption.
Create the direction sheet.
Assemble the bulletin board.

Student Behaviors

Students read the phrases and pick out the animal word.

Students write the words they find on a piece of notebook
    paper and have them checked.

Specific Examples

Among the Valentine greetings found in the magazine article
    are the following:
    Seal it with a kiss.
    I'll bee yours.
    I'd be lion if I said I didn't love you.
    I go-pher you.
    I can't bear to be without you.
    You're robin me if you won't be mine.
    Won't you be my ladybug?

Unexpected Outcomes

A third grade teacher whose class was studying animal
    classification had her students indicate the classification
    as well.
A practice teacher was stumped with the phrase "Huffin' and
    puffin' for you."

Circus Information

Materials
Illustrations of circus animals and characters
Construction paper
Felt-tip pens
Opaque projector
Encyclopedia set or other resource materials about the circus

Procedures

Read through the resource material available
Select a number of questions suitable for students' ability
Enlarge circus animal and character illustrations. Color them.
   (1 for each question)
Cut a large circle from a light colored construction paper,
   and label it "Center Ring"

Student Behaviors

Students read the questions, select any one that appeals to
   them, and find the answer in the resource materials.
   Working in any sequence the student desires, he answers
   all questions. The student should be sure to number his
   answer sheet to match the question numbers. When the
   student has successfully answered all questions, his
   name is written by the teacher in the "Center Ring."

Specific Examples

The objective was to encourage third and fourth graders to
   gain confidence in using encyclopedias. The ten questions were based on information found in *Worldbook*
   circus article.
   1. When and where did the modern circus develop?
   2. How many large circuses toured the U.S. in the late
          1800's?
   3. Who owned the greatest show on earth?
   4. How did young boys earn tickets to the circus?
   5. What were circus tents called?
   6. How does the band help the circus?
   7. What might you see in a side show?
   8. What do you call the men who unload the equipment
          and set it up?
   9. What do the circus winter quarters look like?
   10. What kind of act made each of these people famous:
          (a) Emmett Kelly, (b) Clyde Beatty, (c) Unus,
          (d) the Wallenda Family?

Unexpected Outcomes

One fourth grade boy, having completed #4, grinned and said, "They earned tickets by watering the hefalumps and woozles." We had a good laugh.

The concept of subheadings within informational articles became clearer to students because as they worked through the questions they began turning to the proper sections rather than merely flipping all pages at random.

Kite Flying

Materials

Construction paper in assorted colors
Felt pen
Resource information about kites, kite flying, and historic and scientific uses of them

Procedures

Read through resource material selecting facts for questions.
Cut kites of various sizes and colors so that there is one for each question.
Using felt pen, write one question on each kite.
Number the questions (kites).
Post the kites.
Set up the reserve shelf for student use.

Student Behaviors

Students will seek answers to question in the resource
materials.
Answers will be written and turned in to classroom teacher or
media specialist for verification.

Specific Examples

Questions might include the following:
1. What is ski kiting?
2. People disagree about who really invented kites.
   Name the two men usually credited with the in-
   vention, and tell where and when they lived.
3. Explain how a kite train is made.
4. How were kites used to build bridges?
5. How were kites used during the Spanish-American
   War?
6. In what country is kite fighting a national sport?
7. How do they arm their kites?
8. Using Bartlett's *Familiar Quotations*, find a quotation
   about kites. Who said it?

9. Explain how a kite flies. Draw a diagram to help explain the process.
10. Who invented a box kite? Where and when?

Unexpected Outcomes

The art department developed a kite building and flying project that was coordinated with this bulletin board activity.

A grade level competition quiz program based on the information required to answer the bulletin board questions was developed in the classrooms.

National Wildlife Week
(Net a Pet)

Materials

Drawings of four people holding butterfly nets
Construction paper in assorted colors
Felt-tip pens
List of endangered species
Opaque projector
Sheet of paper for directions
5 x 8 cards
Books on animals

Procedures

Enlarge or draw four people holding butterfly nets.
Label each net using the terms Birds, Fish, Mammals, and Reptiles/Amphibians.

From the list of endangered species, select an appropriate
   number being sure to include some from each of the four
   animal types.
Type each animal's name on a separate card, to be scattered
   among the people on the board.
Type direction sheet and post it.
Cut letters for caption and post it.

Student Behaviors

The caption tells the students to "net a pet." To do this they
   divide their answer sheets into four sections labeled with
   the same four categories that are on the nets.
Students read the names of the species on each card and
   list them under the appropriate heading on the answer
   sheet.
If needed, the student consults the animal books to help him
   determine the correct category of animals unfamiliar to
   him.
Student turns in his answer sheet for correction.

Specific Examples

The following species were used with the third and fourth
   grade students:
   Birds: Eskimo curlew, Canada goose, Sandhill crane,
      Brown pelican, Whooping crane, California con-
      dor, and Whip-poor-will
   Fish: Sturgeon and Stickleback
   Mammals: Kangaroo rat, Indiana bat, timber wolf, Mana-
      tee (sea cow), Eastern cougar, Prairie dog, and
      Sonoran pronghorn
   Reptiles/Amphibians: Blunt-nosed leopard lizard, Hous-
      ton toad, Puerto Rican boa, and American alligator

Unexpected Outcomes

Students discovered that the first word in the animal's name
   was not always the word to use in an index. The key-
   word concept became clearer.

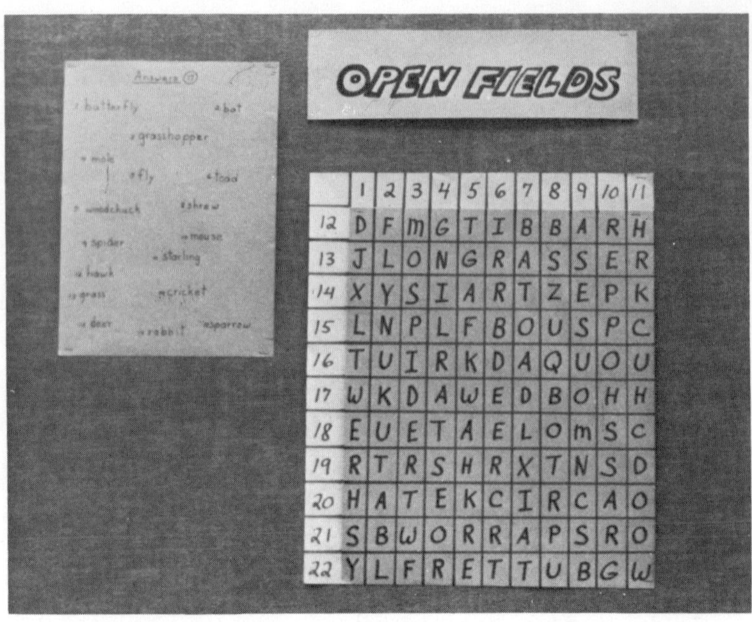

Hidden-Word Puzzle
for National Wildlife Week

Materials

Three hidden-word puzzles which are publications of National Wildlife Federation for the 1975 observance of National Wildlife Week
Felt-tip pens (contrasting colors)
Construction paper (6 sheets—2 each of blue, green, and yellow)
Sheet of paper for directions
Primary typewriter

Procedures

Mark off 3 sheets of construction paper (one of each color) in 12 rows and 12 columns.

34

In the first row of each sheet, write the numbers 1 through 11 placing 11 in the extreme right hand column.

In the left hand column, write the numbers 12 through 22 placing 22 at the bottom. This leaves the square in the upper left hand corner blank.

Using a pen of a contrasting color, copy the letters onto the grid using the N.W.W. publication as a guide.

Use the blue grid for the water habitat, the green for woodlands, and the yellow for open fields.

Print the animal name answer words on a matching sheet of construction paper for posting beside the puzzle grid. Captions identifying the habitats should also be in the matching color.

Posters or wildlife pictures may be used for added interest.

Student Behaviors

The student is asked to copy animal names onto a piece of paper.

The student locates the words on the grid. Words may be spelled vertically, horizontally, or diagonally, all going in either direction.

To prove he has located the word on the grid, the student
writes the numbers for the row and column to identify
the position of the *first* letter of the word. (This is similar
to the use of letters and numbers on maps).

Specific Examples

Animal name answer words used for open fields included:
butterfly, bat, grasshopper, mole, fly, toad, woodchuck,
shrew, spider, mouse, starling, hawk, cricket, deer,
rabbit, and sparrow.

Unexpected Outcomes

Included in the packet of materials from National Wildlife
Federation were iron-on patches which were used as
prizes. (Out of approximately 100 students who could
have completed the puzzles, about 30 completed all three
and became eligible for the patch). Students wanted to
know if they did the puzzle additional times could they
not have additional patches.

Countdown to Summer
(Year-End Retrieval of Materials Graph)

Materials

Construction paper in assorted colors
Black felt-tip pen

Procedures

On a strip of white paper placed at the left-hand edge of the
display area, mark off number lines from zero at the bottom to 25 at the top. This strip is the scale for reading
the bar graph. It can also be used as a measure when
creating the individual bars for the graph.
Each classroom has its own bar labeled with the teacher's
name.
Bars are color-coded by grade level, and all of one grade are
posted next to each other.
This facilitates comparison on and between grade levels.
Measure strips of colored construction paper (the bars) to
correspond with the number of items still charged to
that classroom.
Trim the top so that it is pointed.
As materials are returned, the top point of the bar is clipped
off shortening it so that the bar continues to indicate the
number of items outstanding.

Student Behaviors

Graph reading was practiced and students were motivated to
help locate materials signed out to their room.
Classroom groups were proud of 100 percent achieve-
ment.

Unexpected Outcomes

Bar graphs indicating overdues by classroom lose their
effectiveness if continued over an extended period of
time. The goal has to be designed so that rapid visual
changes occur if interest is to be maintained.

Beatrix Potter Project

Materials

Beatrix Potter stories and biographies
Pictures of the animal characters from her books, commercially or self-made 5 x 8 cards
Primary typewriter
Construction paper for letters in caption
Crossword puzzle content
Construction paper and felt-tip pens to make puzzle
Sheet of construction paper for directions
Ditto masters and paper for duplicating a certificate form and for duplicating puzzle answer sheet

Procedures

Place background reading material on Reserve Shelf.
Divide involvement bulletin board into three sections: Part I, Identifying character illustrations; Part II, Peter Rabbit crossword puzzle; Part III, Questions to answer about Miss Potter's life.
Post pictures in first section, puzzle in second section, and cards in the third.
Number the illustrations.

Student Behaviors

Student numbers his paper to correspond with the numbers on the illustrations.
He writes beside each number the character's name and title of the book it is in.

Student completes the Peter Rabbit crossword puzzle answer
   sheet.
Student answers questions about Miss Potter's life. Refers to
   references as necessary.
Student turns in answer sheets for correction.
Those who correctly answered all three parts receive a certificate.

Specific Examples

The illustrations of characters to be identified included: Peter
   Rabbit, Tailor of Gloucester, Mrs. Tiggy Winkle, Jemima
   Puddleduck, Jeremy Fisher, Mrs. Rabbit, the Owl from
   Squirrel Nutkin, Two Bad Mice, Benjamin Bunny, Squirrel
   Nutkin, Tom Kitten.
Questions for Part III included:
   1. When and where was Miss Potter born?
   2. What was the name of her farm?
   3. Did she have any brothers or sisters?
   4. If so, what were their names?
   5. When was *Peter Rabbit* first published?
   6. Did she ever marry, and if so, when and to whom?

Unexpected Outcomes

There was much interest in this activity, and the music teacher
prepared with fourth grade children a Peter Rabbit musical which was presented for the rest of the school, and
again at an evening performance for parents.

Transparencies from the *Peter Rabbit Coloring Book* (Dover)
were made and colored and projected as background
scenery for the chorus's presentation.

The musical used was *The Songs of Peter Rabbit Based On
"The Tale of Peter Rabbit" By Beatrix Potter*. Words and
music by Dudley Glass. Frederick Warne & Co., Ltd.:
(London and New York), 1951.

Peter Rabbit Crossword Puzzle

Clues

Across:

1. What Mr. McGregor hung Peter's clothes up to scare
2. Peter went to Mr. McGregor's ______
3. The first thing Peter ate
4. She went to get brown bread and buns
5. She took a ______ and her umbrella
6. Peter's father was put into a ______
7. Peter's third sister's name
8. Peter's second sister's name
9. He lost the first one in the cabbages
10. What the cat was staring at

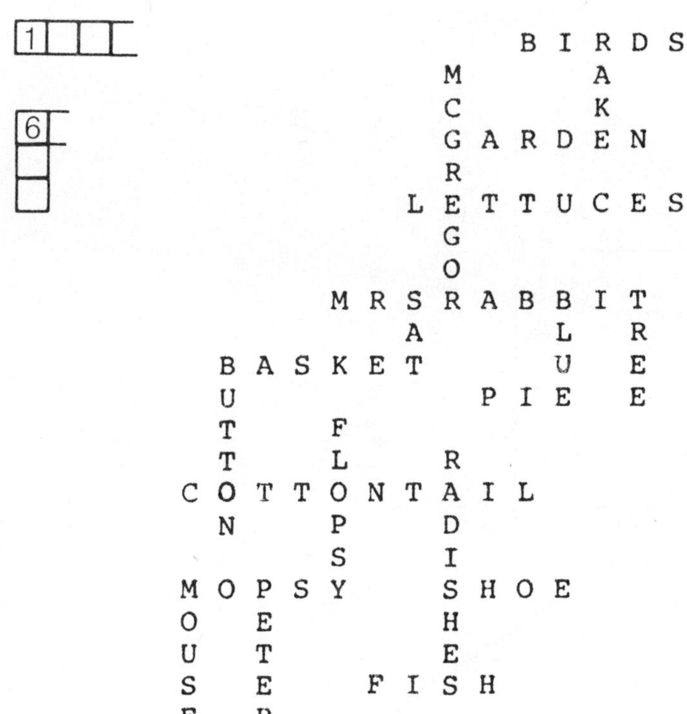

Down:

1. She ran in and out carrying peas and beans in her mouth
2. Peter was caught by it in a gooseberry net
3. The rabbit who did not mind his mother
4. Peter's first sister's name
5. What Peter did to rest, or what the cat did to watch the fish
6. He chased Peter
7. What Peter ate that made him sick
8. The color of Peter's jacket
9. What Mr. McGregor waved as he ran
10. Peter and his family lived under a fir _______

This is awarded to

____

for successfully completing the

Beatrix Potter Bulletin Board

Rolling Terrace Media Center

Oct. 28, 1974

M. Ellen Jay

Winnie the Pooh

Materials

Primary typewriter
Ditto master and paper for duplicating answer sheets
Construction paper—assorted colors for map and puzzle; black for silhouettes
Felt-tip pens
Sheet of paper for map questions
Opaque projector
World of Pooh, for endpaper map; *House At Pooh Corner*, for character silhouettes

Procedures

Using black construction paper, make enlarged silhouettes of Pooh characters.
Whatever scale is used, Christopher Robin is about three times as tall as Piglet.

Develop crossword puzzle. (Suggestions for doing this appear in the Techniques Section, p. 12 .)

Cut strips of construction paper 2" wide and mark off 2" squares with felt-tip pen.

These strips are then positioned to provide puzzle spacing as required.

Answer squares are numbered and directional arrows added.

Print or type the "Across" and "Down" clues on additional sheets of construction paper.

Students are able to work more easily when directional arrows are used for "Across" and "Down" in conjunction with the clue number on the actual puzzle. (See diagram on puzzle example in Beatrix Potter board directions.)

Silhouettes are placed on the board as a border for the puzzle section.

Recreate the map from the endpapers in scale for your display area. Use the opaque projector and enlarge the endpaper drawings, or create your own trees, house, stream, etc.

Devise questions to emphasize north, south, east, west concepts.

Type or print these questions on a sheet of paper to be placed on map section of board.

Draw and duplicate answer sheets for the crossword puzzle.

Student Behaviors

Students will use answer sheets to work out crossword puzzle answers.

Students will number a sheet of paper to correspond with the map question numbers and answer the questions.

Students will turn in answer sheets for checking.

Specific Examples

Crossword puzzle questions:

Across
1. Where the bees keep their honey, or what Tiggers don't climb
2. The bear of very little brain's full name
3. The name Pooh lived under
4. What Eeyor lost

5. The real person in the stories
6. Pooh and Piglet walked around the tree tracking this animal
7. It was in his door that Pooh got stuck
8. What Pooh tried to look like to fool the bees
9. Trading places with Roo got him a bath and some medicine
10. These stories took place in the 100 Aker _______ .

Down

1. She gave Piglet a bath
2. Pooh's favorite thing to eat
3. He is the gloomy one
4. Pooh made up a _______ as he went along
5. The new game was called Pooh _______
6. The way Owl spells his name
7. Pooh built a trap for one of these
8. Kanga's baby's name
9. He eats every thing except honey, hay corns, and thistles
10. What surrounded Piglet

```
                        T  R  E  E
         K                          E
         A                          Y
W  I  N  N  I  E  T  H  E  P  O  O  H
         G                    R     U
      S  A  N  D  E  R  S           M
                     T
            T  A  I  L
                     C                    R
                     K     W              O        T
         C  H  R  I  S  T  O  P  H  E  R  R  O  B  I  N
            O              L     E              G
            N                    F              E
W  O  O  Z  L  E                 F              R
            Y                 R  A  B  B  I  T
                                 L
                        C  L  O  U  D        W  O  O  D
                                 M           A
                              P  I  G  L  E  T
                                             E
                                             R
```

PART II: **Map Questions** were the following types:
1. What direction would Pooh walk if he left his house to visit Piglet?
2. It is west of Eeyor's house, east of the Hefalump Trap, south of the Bee Tree, and north of the Swampy Place? Ans. 100 Aker Wood

Unexpected Outcomes

Some second graders did the project.

One third grader asked why none of this was done "last year." Obviously, he did not recognize what was called for, or the projects had been of no interest to him the previous year. Involvement bulletin boards had been posted frequently.

Word Recognition
Using a Familiar Poem

Materials

Many copies of the poem
5 x 8 cards for typing poem lines
Primary typewriter
Construction paper for caption letters
Holiday wrapping paper

Procedures

Type no more than four lines to the card
Number cards in sequence to aid reader following lay-out
Leave out two words per card, but not always the obvious
  rhyming word
Cover (or border) the display area with colorful wrapping
  paper printed with an appropriate motif
Place cards on board

Student Behaviors

Using a piece of notebook paper, the student writes down the
  missing words in sequence.
He reads the stanza on the card, locates it in the poem and
  fills in the missing words.

Specific Examples

Twas the night before Christmas,
When all through the -----

Not a creature was stirring,
Not even a -----.

The stockings were hung
By the-------with care,
In hopes that Saint Nicholas
---- would be there.

Unexpected Outcomes

A student with limited reading skills can fill in the blank even
if he can't read all the words. He can locate the "missing"
one and copy it.

Kite Poems

Materials

Assorted colors of construction paper
Felt-tip pens
Poetry collection

Procedures

Select poetry that has to do with kite flying.
Create a caption: KITES, PLUS WIND, PLUS MARCH
EQUALS POETRY (Can use math symbols.)
Cut varying sizes of paper kites from construction paper.
Use larger kites for longer poems.
Print poems on the kites.

Place kites on the board or display area.
Post a directions sheet.

Student Behaviors

Student reads poems.
Student locates additional poems related to the theme.
Student copies these poems onto additional kites.
Student writes his own poem to use on a kite.

Specific Examples

Typical of poems we used are the following:

> I am a kite high in the sky,
> Floating along with the wind,
> And the funniest thing
> I'm holding a string,
> With a boy on the other end.
>
> *Collum*

> A kite is never just a kite.
> It's a pennant that a boy
> sends up by means of
> string and wind
> To advertize his joy.
>
> *Marcellino*

> A kite, a sky, and a good firm breeze,
> And acres of ground away from trees,
> And 100 yards of clean strong string—
> Oh boy, O boy!
> I call that Spring.
>
> *Sawyer*

A B C Poem

Materials

Three reprint posters of the poem "The Alphabet." (F. E. Compton Co., Department of Educational Services, 425 North Michigan Avenue, Chicago, Illinois, 60611)
4 x 6 cards
Felt pens, or
Primary typewriter

Procedures

Display the posters at a height students can read easily.
Type or print questions on 4 x 6 cards.
Post questions with the poem posters.

Student Behaviors

Student reads through the poem, then reads a question.

Student locates the phrase in the poem that answers the
   question. The answer will be an alphabet letter name.
Student continues in this manner until all questions are
   answered.
Student turns in paper to be checked.

Specific Examples

Questions are created by citing phrases from the poem in
   the following manner:
   1. This letter looks like a half-melted snowman. (B)
   2. This letter grew a moustache. (G)
   3. This letter is a leg with a very long shoe. (L)
   4. This letter makes twin mountains. (M)
   5. This letter is a ribbon tied into a bow. (R)
   6. This letter is a leg dancing a jig. (Z)

Unexpected Outcomes

The activity gave students a new way of looking at letter
   shapes, and they began making up their own questions
   and definitions.

Mother Goose, Mother Goof

Materials

Mother Goose rhymes
Strips of two contrasting colors of construction paper
Felt-tip pens

Set of nursery rhyme pictures
Construction paper for letters for caption

Procedures

Choose rhymes.
Print the first line of a rhyme on one strip of paper and the
  second line on a strip of contrasting color. (All first lines
  will be on one color paper; all second lines the other.)
If nursery rhyme pictures are used, place the first lines
  next to the pictures they go with.
After posting pictures and first lines, place second line strips
  on the board so that matching first and second lines are
  not adjacent.
Number the second line strips.
Create and post direction sheet.
Create and post caption.

Student Behaviors

Students will match the correct first line with the correct second line.
There will be an even number of strips and they match per-
  fectly.
The students write the first line on their paper, and after it they
  place the number for the correct second line.
The student completes all the examples and has paper
  checked.

Specific Examples

Rhymes included: Hey Diddle-diddle, Hickory Dickory Dock,
  Jack and Jill, Humpty Dumpty, Old Mother Hubbard, Old
  Woman Who Lived in a Shoe, Old King Cole, Little Miss
  Muffet, and Tom, Tom the Piper's Son.
These rhymes were chosen as they matched a commercial
  picture set.

Unexpected Outcomes

Older students seemed to enjoy doing the matching mentally.

What Story Do I Live in?

Materials

White construction paper
Felt pens in assorted colors
Opaque projector
Collection of picture books to provide illustrations for enlarging
OPTIONAL: Laminating materials and equipment

Procedures

Leaf through picture books identifying specific pictures for enlarging.
There should be one picture per book.
Enlarge illustrations by using the opaque projector process.
Because these pictures are potentially reusable, they are worth laminating.
Make the caption.
Post the pieces on the bulletin board.

Student Behaviors

Because this activity is geared to the youngest children in the school, there is no writing of the answers. The children discuss the pictures and talk about the characters among themselves, or the teacher may take a group into the area and hold a group discussion.

Specific Examples

Distinctive illustrations may be found in popular books such as the following:
Cats For Sale
Mike Mulligan And His Steam Shovel
Petunia
Three Little Pigs
Three Bears
Three Billy Goats Gruff

Curious George
Are You My Mother?

Unexpected Outcomes

The older children have fun recognizing old friends.
From time to time, fabric stores offer colorful materials featuring book illustrations or characters. These fabrics may be used successfully as wall hangings to develop interest in the book from which the characters come. When purchasing lengths of fabric for this purpose, one must be sure to have sufficient length to include the full pattern repeat, allow for hemming, and also allow for turning the edge over a wooden frame and tacking it. Frames can be made from strips of 1 x 2 furring available at lumber yards, strengthened at the corners with small angle irons. Corners do not need to be morticed for these frames.

54

Animal of the Month

Materials

Animal stories from Fiction collection
Construction paper—light, bright color for background and
    black for animal silhouettes
Supply of 3 x 5 cards
Black felt-tip pen for lettering poster
Opaque projector

Procedures

Create the silhouettes enlarging pictures by means of
    opaque projection technique.
Cut out and mount silhouette on construction paper.
Label with caption: (Name of animal) STORIES WE HAVE
    READ.
Put up one animal for the month and as students read stories
    about that animal, place student's name, book title and
    author on a 3 x 5 card and post these cards near the
    silhouette poster.

Student Behaviors

Student notes what animal is posted and selects stories to read.

Student uses card catalog to locate stories about specific animals.

Student asks for suggestions from media center personnel.

Student reads stories suggested by cards already posted.

Student reads a book and then discusses the story with media center personnel to verify his having read the story.

Student supplies media center personnel with the information needed for the 3 x 5 card.

Specific Examples

Animals used were: Rabbit, horse, dog, bear, mouse, and cat.

Any animal for which enough stories are available in the collection may be used.

Unexpected Outcomes

When several students read the same story, only one title-author card was used and additional student names were added to it. (This solved a space problem!)

Be prepared to deal with the problem of having several animals in the same story, and animal stories in the collection for which no poster was made.

Author/Title Crossword Puzzle

Materials

Construction paper (3 colors)
Felt-tip pens
Reading list of authors and titles
Ditto master and paper for duplicating answer sheets

Procedures

Follow the directions for constructing crossword puzzles given in the section on techniques. Be sure to include the author's name in the clues.
Print the two clue sheets, the one for "Across" and the other for "Down."
Create answer sheet on ditto master and make enough copies for each student.

Student Behaviors

Student uses prepared answer sheet and works puzzle.
Student uses his prior reading, a reading list, or searches the card catalog for answers.

Specific Examples

This puzzle was designed to stimulate fourth graders to read books on a specific book list. Clues follow:

Across
1. Edmonds tells a story about a _______ gun the children use to scare away Indians.
2. In Selden's story this animal's best friends are a mouse, a cat, and a boy.
3. This is the planet Miss Pickerell goes to in a story by MacGregor.
4. Lindgren tells a story about a little girl whose last name is almost as funny as her adventures.
5. In Lewis's story the children discover a magic kingdom by going through one of these.

6. Cleary wrote a story about a mouse and a _______.
7. Bradbury tells about two children who get stranded on one of these when their boat floats away on the tide.
8. He and his grandmother think the people upstairs are _______, and Rosenbaum tells how they attempt to capture them.

Down
1. Williams tells about Danny's troubles when he tries to use a machine to do his _______.
2. What kind of tree did the space ship land under in Slobodkin's story?
3. Some brave Norwegian children save the _______ by smuggling it past the Germans on their sleds.
4. Gage tells of the adventures shared by two cousins and a _______ during a summer of magic.
5. When words appear here Wilber is saved according to a story by E. B. White.
6. Thurber tells about a sick princess who will not get well until she has the _______ on a chain around her neck.
7. Estes tells of a girl who says she has 100 _______ in her closet, but chooses to wear the same one every day.
8. In this story by Atwater, we meet Mr. Popper and his _______.

Unexpected Outcomes

Not only were avid readers motivated by this puzzle, but a group of least able readers worked with a reading resource teacher and the librarian and completed the puzzle in record time. Students began to race each other to complete the puzzle.

```
                        M A T C H L O C K
                                H
                                O
                C R I C K E T   M
        M A R S               W
        A                     O
        P                     R
        P L O N G S T O C K I N G
        L                 T           M       W
        E           W A R D R O B E   O       E
                            E         P       B
                            A
          M       D         S
        M O T O R C Y C L E U
          O       R         R
          N       E         E
                  S
                  I S L A N D
                  S
K I D N A P P E R S
          E
          N
          G
          U
          I
          N
          S
```


```
```

Bulletin Board Bingo
(Follow-up Activity for a Reading List)

Materials

5 x 8 cards
Primary typewriter
Ditto masters and paper for reproducing reading lists and
    Bingo answer strips
Reading list
Construction paper for caption

Procedures

Create a master for the reading list and duplicate it.
Cut letters for caption and post it.
Create a clue for each title on the reading list, and type
    the clue on a card. (Store clue cards for posting one
    each day.)
Create a master for the answer strips. Duplicate copies. (Five
    rows of 5 boxes.)
Cut strips horizontally so that each student will have a strip of
    5 boxes.
Fill in the strips by writing or typing a single title in each box.
Make sure that no two strips are identical, although there
    will be some overlapping of titles. One way is to begin by
    using all the titles on the list once. Then use every second
    title all the way through, every third title, every fifth title,
    etc.
Begin the game by distributing answer strips and posting
    the first clue.
Add a clue daily leaving up previous clues.

Student Behaviors

Students will begin to read from the list unaware that the
    game is going to be used.
When the game is begun, each student receives his own
    unique answer strip.

If there is a title on his strip he has not yet read, he reads it.

The game is played by the student reading the daily clue, figuring out the title represented, checking his own answer strip to see if it is on the strip and coloring in the box if it is.

When all five squares are colored, the student has achieved "Bingo."

By the end of the clue posting everyone should have achieved "Bingo."

Specific Examples

Sample answer strips:

Seal Pup	Kildee House	Popcorn Patch	Two On An Island	Gull Number 737
The Grizzly	Rascal	Bristle Face	Brady	The Loner
Seal Pup	Popcorn Patch	Gull Number 737	Rascal	Brady

Sample clues:

In what book does a spider spin words in her web?

Two children borrowed their grandparents' rowboat when they arrived ahead of schedule.

Unexpected Outcomes

The game was being played simultaneously by 3rd and 4th graders using different reading lists and clues. Each played the other's game, but without answer strips.

Read Your Way
Across the USA

Materials

Set of at least fifty-two 5 x 8 cards
Pressure sensitive labels ¾ x 1½ inch size
Standard size typewriter
Construction paper for caption
Outline map of the USA, showing state lines, to fit display area

Procedures

Create two index cards. This is done by typing the number 1 through 50 in columns on a card. The names of the states are listed after the numbers but by geographic regions. One through 6 will be New England; 7 through 12 for Mid-Atlantic, etc.

On the second card type an alphabetical listing of the states and follow each state by the number from the first index

card. These indexes aid students who wish to locate a
specific suggestion rather than flip through all 50 cards.
Next, number a set of cards 1 through 50. The labels will be
placed on these cards.
Go through the fiction collection selecting books for which
a specific state setting can be identified. For these books,
type a pressure sensitive label giving author and title.
Affix the label to the corresponding card. It helps if labels
are placed alphabetically by author, but obviously addi-
tions prevent complete alphabetizing.
Post outline map and caption.

Student Behaviors

Student selects a title from the reading list and upon completion of the book is permitted to color in the state
associated with that book. A large map for an entire class
can be used in a competitive situation with other classrooms of the same grade each class having its own map.
It is also workable to give individual students who are
sufficiently interested their own outline maps to complete.

Specific Examples

Rabbit Hill by Lawson (Connecticut)
Stuart Little by White (New York)
Kildee House by Montgomery (California)
Piney Woods by Cotton (Florida)

Unexpected Outcomes

This format can be used to highlight international themes.
Be prepared to deal with stories in which the characters
travel through several states; e.g., *Down the Mississippi*
by Bulla or *Hemi, A Mule* by Brenner.
One possible solution is to label a card "0" for Multi-state
Travel. Allow the student credit for just one of the states
included.

Can You Name
the Product Advertised?

Materials

List of advertising slogans taken from magazines subscribed
to in the media center
Construction paper in assorted colors
Felt-tip pens
Sheet of paper for directions
Slips of white paper

Procedures

Print each advertising slogan, omitting the product name, on
strips of colored construction paper. Vary the colors.
Number each strip.
Place strips randomly on the bulletin board.
Make direction sheet and post it.
Create caption and post it.

(Note: It is advisable to avoid using slogans for tobacco, alcohol,
personal products, etc. to avoid value judgment complaints.)

Student Behaviors

Student numbers his paper to correspond with the number
of product slogans posted.
Student writes the product name beside the appropriate
number.
Student completes the project and turns paper in for checking.

If his answers are correct, his name is printed on a slip of
white paper and posted on the bulletin board among the
slogans.

Specific Examples

Fly the friendly skies of _______.
Buy a piece of the Rock.
Umm, umm, good!
One good crunch deserves another.
Join the _______ generation.

Unexpected Outcomes

It became important to the student to be allowed to choose the
location for posting his name slip. The vicinity of a soft
drink was more prestigious than that of dog food!
More non-readers stayed in during free time to work on this
board than any other one used to date.

Word and Phrase Origins

Materials

Books for a reserve shelf that provide phrase origins. (Those
by Funk, Asimov, and Morris are especially useful).
Primary typewriter
3 x 5 cards
File box

Procedures

Type individual phrases on cards (one per card).
Place cards in file box.
Create reserve shelf.
Type a direction sheet and post it with file box and books.

Student Behaviors

Student will select a card from the file box choosing one that
intrigues him.
Student will then search books to find that word or phrase
origin.
Student will paraphrase the description in his own words,
and indicate where he found the explanation by giving
book title, author, and page.
The student's written work will be checked by the classroom
teacher.

Specific Examples

The teacher creating the file box should make sure that the
phrases included are those that would be of most interest
and significance to the students.

Corduroy road	Dungaree
Sandwich	Candid camera
The real McCoy	Give you the creeps
Silhouette	Let the cat out of the bag
Funnybone	Free lance

Unexpected Outcomes

Students usually have not discovered this type of book and they find them interesting and sometimes amusing.

Black History

Materials

1 biography for each person represented. (The Crowell Easy Reading Biography Series is especially good for younger students).
1 sheet of plain paper
Felt pen, or
Primary typewriter

Procedures

Go through the biography collection and choose books appropriate to the reading level of participating students.
Place these books on a reserve shelf.
Type a list of occupations matching those of the biographies.
Post the list near the reserve shelf.

Student Behaviors

s copy the occupations list onto their answer sheet.
Students examine the reserved books and determine the occupation of each biographee.
Students write the person's name beside the proper occupation and turn in the answer sheets for checking.

Specific Examples

Some of the people and occupations used included the following:

    Cowboy—Nate Love
    Basketball player—Wilt Chamberlain
    Poet—Langston Hughes
    Baseball player—Jackie Robinson
    Photographer—Gordon Parks
    Doctor—Charles Drew
    Musician—Louis Armstrong
    Singer—Marion Anderson

Unexpected Outcomes

It was difficult to keep the books on the reserve shelf as students wanted to check out the books immediately.

I. Bicentennial Celebration
Crostic Puzzle
(Adapt for on-going use)

Materials

Construction paper (red, white, and blue)
Felt-tip pens
Sheet of paper for directions
Ditto master and paper for copying answer sheet
Primary typewriter
Sketch of Bicentennial emblem

Procedures

Enlarge the emblem.
Cut strips of paper and mark into squares so that the number
of squares and the number of letters in the expected
answer match.
Post these strips in the sequence of the clues on the clue
sheet.
Type out directions for working the puzzle and post them on
the board.
Create a ditto master copy of the answer strips posted on the
board and make copies for all students.
Create caption and post it.

Student Behaviors

Student writes his answers on the prepared answer sheet.
Student reads a clue and checks the corresponding answer
line to determine the number of letters in the answer.
Student is informed that if all questions are answered correctly, the initial letters will spell BICENTENNIAL CELE-
BRATION.
The student knows the number of letters in the answer and
the initial letter.
If he does not know the answer he has these clues to assist
him search atlases and other reference material for the
answers he needs.

Specific Examples

Clues and answers follow:

1. Site of Tea Party ------   Boston
2. 29th state to join the union ----   Iowa
3. The Fundamental Orders, written in this state, later served as a model for the Constitution -----------   Connecticut
4. National emblem (bird) -----   Eagle
5. This is the name of both a city and a state --- ----   New York
6. The Alamo is in this state -----   Texas
7. Nickname for the state of Washington ---------   Evergreen
8. Birthplace of jazz music & biggest city in Louisiana --- -------   New Orleans
9. Where Mt. Washington is located --- ---------   New Hampshire
10. Boise is the capitol city of this state -----   Idaho
11. Largest state in the Union ------   Alaska
12. Capitol city of Michigan -------   Lansing
13. State bird for six different states --------   Cardinal
14. This coast is bordered by the Atlantic Ocean ----   East
15. Nickname for the state of Texas ---- ----   Lone Star
16. New York was the -------- state to join the Union   Eleventh
17. Maryland's state flower ----- ---- -----   Black-eyed Susan
18. Smallest state in the Union ----- ------   Rhode Island
19. Capital city of Georgia -------   Atlanta
20. Number of original colonies --------   Thirteen
21. They lived here first -------   Indians
22. The Buckeye state ----   Ohio
23. The colonies formed a new ------   Nation

Unexpected Outcomes

Teachers had as much fun with this activity as the students. They would be seen working it out before and after school.

II. Bicentennial Celebration

(Adapt for on-going use)

Materials

Construction paper colored red, white, and blue
3 x 5 cards
Felt pens, red and blue
Resource materials
Primary typewriter
Typing paper

Procedures

Cut strips of construction paper sized 8″ x 18″. These should be
red and blue, the color mix depending upon the layout
to be used.
Print questions on cards, one per card. For questions to be
mounted on red paper, write in blue. For questions to be
mounted on blue paper, write in red.

Place 5 cards on each strip of construction paper.
Number the strips 1 through 10.
Type direction sheets.
Post all pieces.
Create reserve materials shelf.

Student Behaviors

Students will write answers to questions on notebook paper.
Students may earn up to 200 points by correctly identifying
the importance of each topic listed on the question cards.
Students will turn in written answers to scorer. (The scorer
will grant up to four points for each answer depending
upon the completeness of the student's answer).

Specific Examples

The five question cards on each strip are related by theme,
such as the following:

WOMEN
1. Betsy Ross
2. Molly Pitcher
3. Barbara Fritchie
4. Clara Barton
5. Harriet Tubman

MEN
1. Ben Franklin
2. Thomas Jefferson
3. Paul Revere
4. John Paul Jones
5. Daniel Boone

EVENTS
1. Boston Tea Party
2. Louisiana Purchase
3. Missouri Compromise
4. The Alamo
5. Attack on Pearl
   Harbor

SYMBOLS
1. Statue of Liberty
2. Liberty Bell
3. Uncle Sam
4. U.S. Flag
5. Elephant and
   Donkey

ANIMALS
1. Bald eagle
2. Beaver
3. Bison
4. Quarter horse
5. Longhorn steer

INVENTORS
1. Alexander Bell
2. Thomas Edison
3. George W. Carver
4. Henry Ford
5. Wright Brothers

TRANSPORTATION
1. Spirit of St. Louis
2. Pony Express
3. Erie Canal
4. Transcontinental R.R.
5. Clipper Ships

WARS
1. French & Indian
2. American Revolution
3. Spanish American
4. War of 1812
5. Civil War

DOCUMENTS
1. Articles of Confederation
2. Declaration of Inde-
   dependence
3. Bill of Rights
4. U.S. Constitution
5. Gettysburg Address

PLACES
1. Lexington and Concord
2. Valley Forge
3. Yorktown
4. Sutter's Fort
5. Attack on Pearl Harbor

Unexpected Outcomes

To be more appealing (less overwhelming) to students, post cards for one strip at a time.

To adapt to grade level differences, students may be instructed to do only cards or topics indicated for them. For example, third graders concentrating on a Colonial Times Unit, did only those items marked with asterisks.

National Park Names in Code

Materials

Outline map of the U.S.
Construction paper
Felt-tip pens
Pictures of the parks (optional)
List of the parks
Yarn or colored string
Sheet of paper for directions

Procedures

On a strip of construction paper print the letters A through Z.
Under these letters write the numbers 1 through 26. This
    creates the code which is posted on the bulletin board.
Translate the list of park names into code and create a strip
    name in code for each park used. It is helpful to use a
    two-color system when numbering, alternating colors.
    This eliminates student's confusion regarding the num-
    bers 1, 2 or 12.
Create a large outline map showing state lines.
Place the code name strips around the outside of the map.
Connect the strips with the geographic location using yarn.
Number the geographic locations.
Cut letters for the caption and post it.
Type direction sheet and post it.
Complete the board layout using park pictures.

Student Behaviors

Student numbers a sheet of paper to correspond with the
    geographic location numbers.
Student breaks the code and writes the name of the park
    after the number.
When all names have been identified, the student turns in his
    paper for correction.

Specific Examples

ACADIA   1 *3* 1 *4* 9 *1*   (Numbers in italic are printed
                                       in a second color)
YELLOWSTONE   25 5 12 *12* 15 *23* 19 *20* 15 *14* 5
EVERGLADES   5 *22* 5 *18* 7 *12* 1 4 5 *19*

Unexpected Outcomes

A fourth grade teacher added requirements for her students
    asking them to name the state as well as to determine the
    name of the national park.

State Shapes

Materials

Outlines of individual states to be enlarged
Opaque projector
Construction paper in assorted colors
Laminating supplies and equipment
Sheet of paper for directions
Reference materials for Reserve Shelf

Procedures

Keep scale consistent. Rhode Island has to be large enough
to see! If Rhode Island is 1/2" by 1½", California, Texas,
and Alaska will exceed a single sheet of construction
paper.
If state shapes are to be laminated, draw as many as possible
on a single sheet of construction paper. Laminate on
both sides before cutting states apart. (The scraps of
laminated paper can be cut into bookmarks and used as

little prizes. In our media center scraps of construction paper salvaged from the paper cutter are used regularly as book marks. Laminated ones become special!)

Post the state shapes randomly in two sections. In the first section include the 25 most distinctive, and therefore easily recognized, state shapes. Place the remaining state shapes in the second section. Place identifying number cards beside each state shape.

Create the caption and post it.

Create direction sheet and post it.

Student Behaviors

This board can be worked on varying levels:

> Level 1: Identify states 1 through 25
> Level 2: Identify states 1 through 50
> Level 3: For the first 25 states, give state name, capitol and the name of one famous person from that state.
> Level 4: Do level 3 for all 50 states

Specific Examples

The series *Enchantment of America* published by Children's Press is very helpful in this project.

Unexpected Outcomes

Special Education students became involved by comparing their wooden state shape puzzle maps (which had state names printed on the parts) with the involvement bulletin board shapes and worked on it for extended periods of time.

Although they could not make the identifications from an atlas page, they could carry around a single puzzle piece until they matched it with the shape on the board.

North, South, East, West
Overhead Projector Game

Materials

Construction paper scraps
Overhead projector

Procedures

Cut out various shapes ranging from one to two inches in
   size.
About 10 different shapes will be needed.
Focus overhead projector onto the chalkboard, mark with
   chalk N at the top, S at the bottom, E at the right, and W
   at the left to identify the cardinal directions.

As the activity proceeds, NE, NW, SE, and SW may be added
at the corners and used to make the game more difficult.
As students gain facility in answering questions, additional
shapes are added to the screen, and this also makes the
game more difficult.

Student Behaviors

Students are seated where they can see the board but not
bump into the projector.
They answer the teacher's questions.
When sufficient skill is achieved, students may create questions to ask other students.

Specific Examples

Possible shapes could be a square, triangle, rectangle,
doughnut, star, leaf, key, hand.
A beginning question with only 3 shapes on the board might
be, "It is north of the leaf, south of the rectangle. What
is it?" Ans. Star.
More complicated questions could be, "East of the star,
south of the rectangle, south of the hand, north of the leaf,
north of the square, and west of the doughnut. What is it?"
Ans. Circle.
Another type of question could be, "What is farthest north-
east?"

Unexpected Outcomes

There is need to identify terminology before the activity is
begun. One person's "doughnut" may be another's
"tire."

Geographic Terms

Materials

Pictures illustrating geographic formations. (Commercial sets
available)
5 x 8 cards for printing definitions and labels
Primary typewriter
Source of definitions; e.g. geographical dictionary, back of
set of pictures, or encyclopedia
Sheet of paper for directions

Procedures

Select pictures and label them with appropriate geographic
term.
Consider the ability of students when wording definitions and
in deciding how many to do.
Type or print definitions on cards for matching with pictures.
Number definition cards.
Place pictures in alphabetic order and definition cards in
numerical order, but make sure that the sequence is mis-
matched.
For intermediate grades, make the number of dashes in the
answer blank on the definition card correspond to the
number of letters in the term. (Use hyphen or space
between strokes of the underscore key.) Post directions
as part of the bulletin board.

Student Behaviors

Student numbers a sheeet of paper to match the number of
items posted.
After reading the definition, the student scans the pictures
and locates the corresponding term which he writes beside
the number on the answer sheet.
Student takes answer sheet to be checked.

Specific Examples

"A rocky, treeless plain where the ground is always frozen is
    called a ------." (Tundra)
"A deep pile of snow that is turned to ice and is slowly moving
    down the mountain is called a -------." (Glacier)
"A big flat area of elevation is called a -------." (Plateau)
"A steep sided channel or river whose banks are mountains
    is called a -----." (Fjord)
"When a river cuts down through rock, what is left is called
    a ------." (Canyon)
"A long row of islands is called an -----------." (Archipelago)

Unexpected Outcomes

Critical thinking leads student to work through the definit-
    tions from the more familiar to the unknown. By the
    process of elimination of the obvious, other answers are
    learned.

Train Toots

Materials

The book *How Engines Talk* by Burleigh. (*Encyclopaedia Britannica* includes signals)
Pictures or drawings of trains
5 x 8 cards
Felt-tip pens
Construction paper
Sheet of paper for directions

Procedures

Create a circuitous train track out of construction paper and trail it about the bulletin board.
With felt-tip pen, using rectangles and squares (see book), create whistle signals.
Number these cards.
At various points along the track, post the cards showing whistle signals. If stations and crossings are pictured, match them up with the signals.
Post pictures of the trains.
Create caption and post it.
Create direction sheet and post it.
Place book on Reserve Shelf.

Student Behaviors

Student will number a piece of paper to correspond with the card numbers.

Student will identify the signals by using the book on the
Reserve Shelf.

Student will write the explanation of the signal beside the
corresponding number.

Student will have answers checked.

Specific Examples

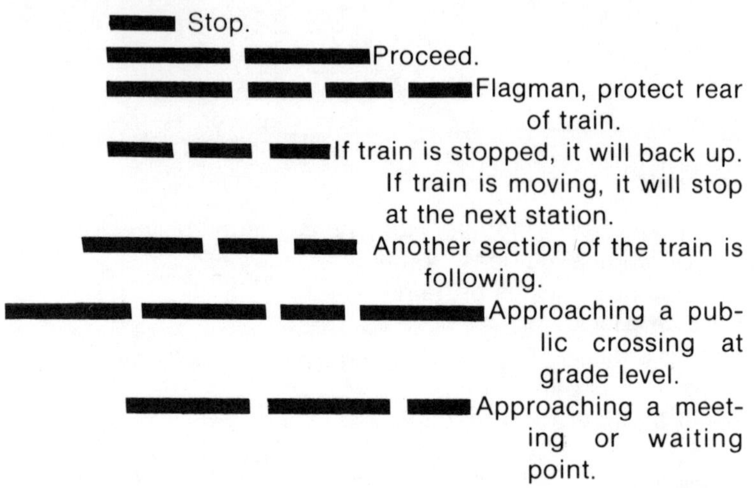

Unexpected Outcomes

Students standing in line began to apply signals to their own
movements.

Animal Footprints

Materials

Construction paper in assorted colors
Black felt-tip pens
Sheet of paper for directions
Opaque projector
Selection of animal books for Reserve Shelf

Procedures

Select approximately 15 distinctive animal footprint illustra-
    tions.
Enlarge these on construction paper of various colors, keep-
    ing scale in mind.
Fill in the footprints with black pen.
Cut freeform sections around the completed tracks.
Randomly post the footprints on the display area.
Identify each footprint with a number.
Create direction sheet and post it.
Create caption and post it.
Place books on Reserve Shelf.

Student Behaviors

Student numbers a piece of paper to match those on the
    bulletin board.
Beside each number the student writes the name of the ani-
    mal that makes that track.
Student uses books on Reserve Shelf to help make identi-
    fications.
The students completing the activity had their names placed
    around the edges of the bulletin board on slips of paper
    made to resemble human footprints.

Specific Examples

Turtle, frog, duck, dog, moose, rabbit, heron, bear, muskrat,
    robin, squirrel, fox, deer, beaver tracks were used.

Unexpected Outcomes

The most popular footprint was that of the frog, possibly
    because a frog was in residence in the media center that
    winter.

Mister Bones

Materials

A skeleton model or diagram
Construction paper
Felt pens
Books on the human skeleton
Bag of bite-sized candy bars individually wrapped for treats ·

Procedures

Display skeleton. (Science model, paper reproduction, or
    self-made diagram)

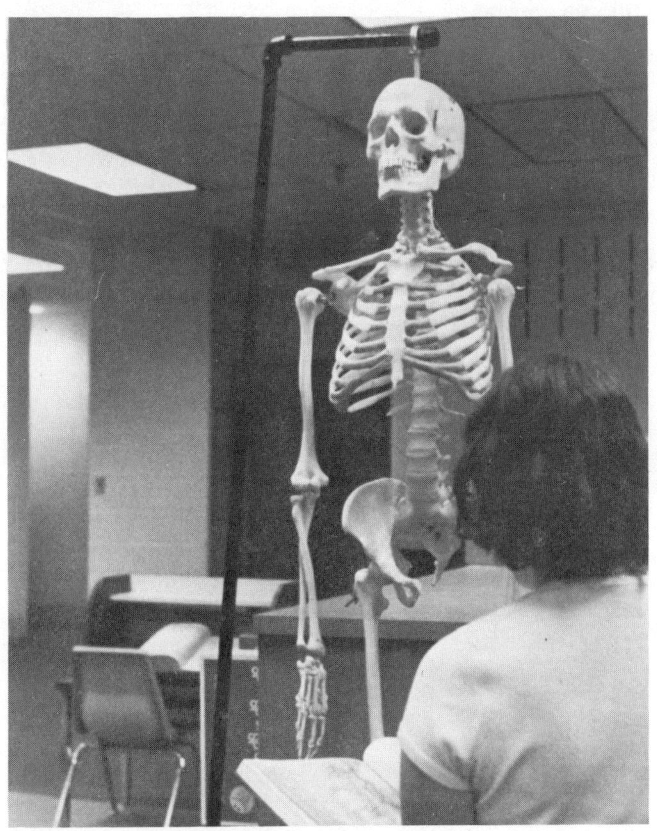

Set up a reserve shelf for reference books.

Make a direction sheet indicating the number of bones to be
identified by students at given grade levels.

Student Behaviors

Student makes a list of bones he chooses to learn according
to his grade level.

In connection with classroom Halloween parties, students
may come to the media center to be tested.

Students identify the specific bones they have learned orally.

Students who identify the required number of bones are
awarded a candy bar "treat."

Specific Examples

Only scientific names are accepted; e.g., patella, not "knee
bone."

Students can practice with each other or individually.

In order to achieve their goal, students must be able to name
the bones on the specified day—not just any day.

Required numbers of bones used were: 3rd grade or below,
10 bones; 4th grade, 15 bones; 5th grade, 20 bones; 6th
grade, 25 bones.

Unexpected Outcomes

Be prepared to hear "spatula" for scapula, and "radiator" for
radius during practice.

Listen in and correct misinformation before it becomes
learned.

Vegetable Soup

Materials

List of vegetables categorized by the parts eaten: leaf, stem,
    root, seed, etc.
Pictures of those vegetables to be enlarged
Opaque projector
Construction paper for caption and vegetable pictures
Sheet of paper for directions
5 x 8 cards cut in half length-wise
Felt-tip pens
Books for reserve shelf

Procedures

Print name of vegetable on half card
Enlarge pictures of vegetables and color them (construction
    paper or felt-tip pens)
Arrange pictures and matching labels randomly on the board.
    Number the labels.
Create caption and post it.
Create direction sheet and post it.
Place books on reserve shelf.

Student Behaviors

Student will divide answer sheet into six sections and label
    each section with a category.
Student will write the name of the vegetable under the proper
    category.
Student will use the Reserve Shelf as necessary.
Student will have answers checked when activity is completed.

Specific Examples

Root: Radish, onion, carrot, potato, beet, turnip, parsnip
Leaf: Lettuce, kale, spinach, chard, cabbage, mustard
Stem: Celery, asparagus, rhubarb
Seed: Rice, pea, corn, lima bean, barley

Seed pod: Squash, cucumber, pepper, green bean, okra,
tomato
Flower bud: Broccoli, artichoke, cauliflower

Unexpected Outcomes

Coordinated with the making of "Stone Soup" in the classroom, students learned something about the vegetables
they contributed.

Weather

Materials

Weather books
White construction paper for clouds, and
Other colors for graphs and charts and the captions, direc-
tions and questions sheets
Primary typewriter
Felt-tip pens
2 Outline maps of the USA 8½ x 11 or slightly larger

Procedures

Place weather books on a Reserve Shelf.
There are six separate activities all relating to weather:

Part 1:
Create a bar graph showing average annual rainfall for five
cities.

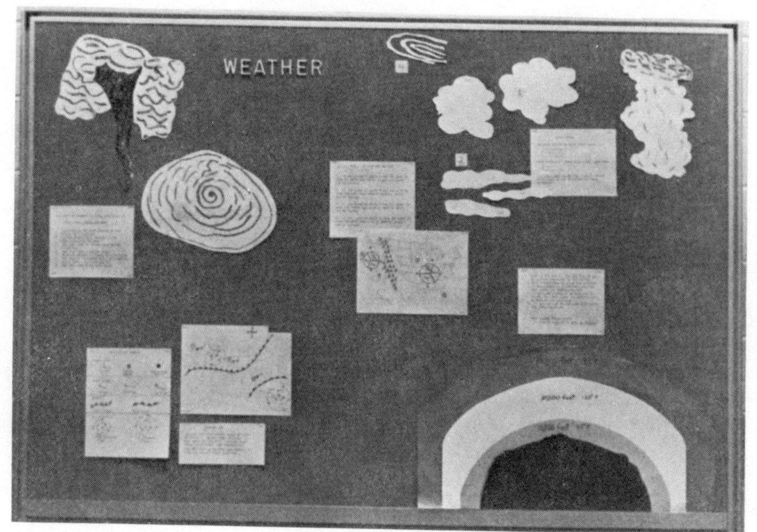

Part 2:

Create a chart showing the temperature of the earth's surface,
   temperature at 10,000 feet altitude, at 30,000 feet, and at
   55,000 feet.

Part 3:

Reproduce two drawings, one showing the structure of a hurricane and one of a tornado. Schematic drawings are
   found in weather books such as *Rain, Hail, Sleet, and
   Snow.*

Part 4:

Make cutouts of five cloud formations. Use page 42 of *The
   First Book of Weather* as a guide.

Part 5:

Create a wind direction and relative weather chart on one of
   the USA outline maps.
Label four locations, such as: 1 in Arizona, 2 in Florida, 3 in
   Iowa, and 4 in northwestern California.

Part 6:

Using basic weather map symbols, create a weather map on the second USA outline map. Make a symbol key to place beside the weather map. Label three points on the map as 1, 2, and 3.

Cut letters for captions.

Specific Examples

Part 1:

Which city gets the most rain?

If you got 20″ of rainfall, in which of the cities would you be living?

How much rainfall does Chicago get?

Part 2:

According to the chart, what is the temperature on the surface of the earth?

If you climbed a 10,000 foot mountain, what would be the temperature at the peak?

If you were flying in an airplane at 30,000 feet, what is the temperature outside?

Part 3:

In the middle of a tornado, is the wind rushing up or down?

Which is bigger—a tornado or a hurricane?

Where does a hurricane start?

Part 4:

Identify three main cloud types.

Combinations of these occur. Name them.

Part 5:

According to the weather map, if you lived at point #1 and the wind is from the south, what kind of weather would you be having?

Part 6:

Symbols included on the weather map are: Cloud cover, wind

speed and direction, warm and cold fronts, high and low
pressure areas.
Observe the three labeled points on the map.
Tell me what the weather would be at point #1. Do the same
for points 2 and 3.
Include cloud cover, wind speed, and temperature.

Bonus question: Are weather and climate the same thing?
Explain.

Mathematics

Timely Questions

Materials

Construction paper circles for clock faces
Felt-tip pens for numbering and drawing hands
5 x 8 cards to type questions
Primary typewriter
Construction paper for letters for captions

Procedures

Cut 14 circles from paper for clock faces (Guides such as
    bottom of wastebasket or top of fish bowl can be used)
Type and number question cards varying word and number
    notations for times
Identify each clock face with a letter near the center
Place the first 10 clock faces in a pyramid formation using a
    base of 4
Include in these the 8 clock faces to answer the first 8 ques-
    tions (The 2 others do not answer any questions but
    eliminate even matching of questions and answers)
The remaining four clock faces *are* matched with their indi-
    vidual questions

Student Behaviors

Student numbers his paper from 1 to 8, and beside each num-
    ber places the letter identification from the clock face
    which answers the question.
Then the student is asked to answer the question 9 through
    12.

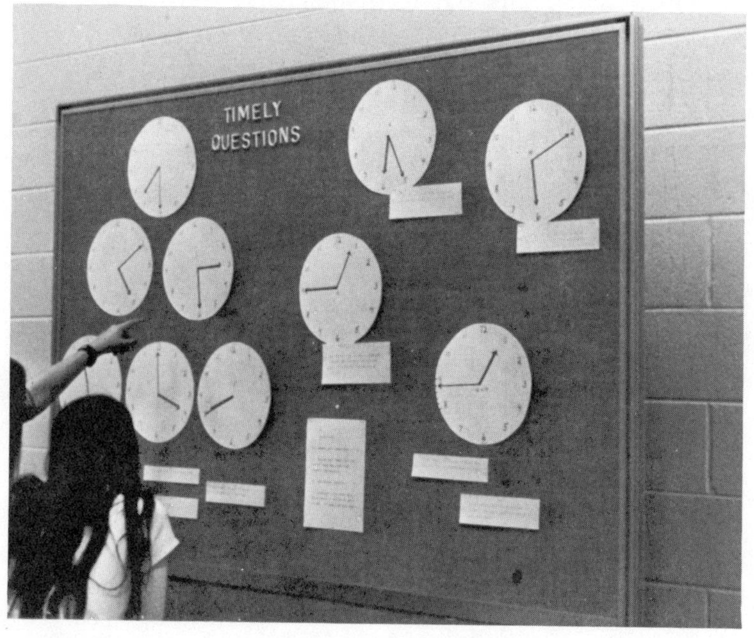

A hint was given on the direction sheet for number 13: "Question 13 is extra hard.
Think about it and try to work it out. It comes out in even number of orbits."

Specific Examples

1. Which clock is at 10:15?
2. Which clock is at seven thirty?
3. Which clock shows twelve o'clock noon?
4. Which clock is at 8:40?
5. If your class eats lunch at 11:30, which clock shows lunch time?
6. Which clock shows the time school starts?
7. If the teachers stay at school one hour after students leave, which clock shows the time teachers leave?
8. Which clock is nearest 5:00?
9. If you eat supper at 6:00 and you are just now getting in, how late are you?

10. If it takes 2½ hours to drive to the beach, and you started at
    4:00, how long until you will be at the beach?
11. If bedtime is usually 8:30 and you are just now going to bed,
    how many extra minutes did you get to stay up?
12. If the rocket blasted off at 6:04, how long have the astro-
    nauts been in space?
13. If it takes one hour and 20 minutes to orbit the earth, how
    many orbits have they made?

Unexpected Outcomes

Even though the hour and minute hands were made signifi-
cantly different in length, until a second color was added
to verify the hour hand there appeared to be confusion
in the students' minds.

Which Is the Better Buy?

Materials

Current grocery store advertising which lists prices and
quantities
Construction paper for background mountings
4 x 6 cards
Felt pens in assorted colors
Primary typewriter

Procedures

To improvise comparison shopping experiences, create a set

of cards which show two quantities of an item and their
respective prices.
These may be done by clipping suitable pictures or sketching
your own.
The current advertising will provide realistic pricings.
Number the cards.
Post the cards.

Student Behaviors

The student will read the information on each card and compute the better buy.
The student will write his answer on notebook paper.
Answer sheets will be turned in to the classroom teacher to be checked.
(The classroom teacher may wish to bring a group to the area to discuss correct answers).

Specific Examples

Compare items such as the following:
1. 20 exposure roll of film with a 36 exposure roll of the same type film.
2. A six pack of returnable 12 ounce beverage bottles with three 1 quart non-returnable bottles of the same beverage.
3. One 10 ounce package of potato chips with two 5 ounce bags of the same brand.
4. Four candy bars for a given price with four of the same candy bars purchased individually.
5. Six ounce frozen concentrated orange juice with a 24 ounce can of ready-to-serve orange juice.

Unexpected Outcomes

Students began to check ounces of ice cream bars for sale in the cafeteria to determine the "better buy."

Around the World
in 80 Words—or less

Materials

Pictures clipped from magazines, or hand drawn sketches
Construction paper in assorted colors
Felt pens in assorted colors
The book *See And Say* by Antonio Frasconi, or others of that
    type.

Procedures

Mount pictures of a single item on construction paper.
Next to the picture, print the words from the four languages
    which name the item pictured.
If there is not sufficient room to put the words on the same
    sheet as the picture, they may be printed on another and
    placed close by.
(The languages in the reference referred to above are English,
    Spanish, French, and Italian. Other languages could be
    used if they were more appropriate for an activity or the
    student body.)
The sequence of the words must be varied, or the students
    will work only from the sense of pattern.

Student Behaviors

Student will divide his answer sheet into four sections, each
    one labeled with the name of one of the languages.
Student will write the words under the proper language name
    heading.

Student will turn in his answer sheet for checking.

Specific Examples

English	*Italian*	*French*	*Spanish*
Light	luce	luminère	luz
Snail	lumaca	escargot	caracol
Sheep	pecora	mouton	oveja
Chair	sedia	chaise	silla
Hat	cappello	chapeau	sombrero

Unexpected Outcomes

When interest is great enough, the students could learn to
say the words correctly.

Borrowed Words

Materials

Construction paper in assorted colors
Felt pens in assorted colors
List of words borrowed from other languages
Primary typewriter
Sheet of plain paper

Procedures

Select the words to be used from the list.
Print them on construction paper sheets or strips.

Number the words.
Create the caption.
Type direction sheet.
Post all the pieces on the bulletin board.

Student Behaviors

Student will copy the word onto a sheet of notebook paper.
Student will use unabridged dictionary or other word book
or language dictionary to find the source of the word.
Student will prepare a final list placing the words under the
name of the language from which we have taken them.
Student will turn in answer sheet for checking.

Specific Examples

Words should be chosen with the students' interests in mind so
that they will be more likely to become interested in the
activity. Words chosen might be associated with a single
type of activity or function, and later another activity
or function could be used to form a series.

Restaurant—French	Pizza—Italian
Pumpernickle—German	Tabasco—Spanish
Hors d'oeuvre—French	Silhouette—French
Babushka—Russian	Chauffeur—French
Goulash—Hungarian	Tambourine—French
Mayonnaise—French	Strudel—German

Unexpected Outcomes

Students learned that in the area of abbreviations a small dif-
ference has a large significance. For example, in the
unabridged dictionary, **fr.** means "from," while **Fr.** means
"French."

Musical Instruments

Materials

Pictures of musical instruments
3x5 cards
Books for Reserve Shelf; phonorecords if second and third
    levels are used
Blank tape
Tape recorder
Record player
Phonorecords to record small excerpts
Construction paper for caption
Felt-tip pens
Sheet of paper for directions
Primary typewriter

Procedures

Make enlargements of pictures of instruments, or use com-
    mercial set.
Be sure to have instruments representing all sections of the
    orchestra.
Cover up labels if the commercial set is already labeled.
Make number cards.
Post pictures and number cards.
Create caption and post it.
Create direction sheet and post it.
Stock the Reserve Shelf according to needs.

The pictures provide opportunity for visual identification
    of musical instruments.
This may be as far as the teacher wishes to go. However, if

tapes are made aural identification on two levels is possible.

A single tape can be produced placing segments in which the instrument is heard unaccompanied on side 1 and as a part of an ensemble on side 2. Each segment should be numbered verbally, but care should be taken not to match the numbers used on the pictures. Neither should the numbering on the two sides of the tape be the same for selections featuring the same instrument.

Student Behaviors

This is a multi-level activity. Students may do only the visual identifications, or they may continue doing the aural identifications on one or two levels. In any case, the answer paper is numbered and the student writes in the name of the instrument he sees or hears. The student will get help from the materials placed on the Reserve Shelf.

Specific Examples

Commercial recordings designed to introduce instrumental sounds to children are available. "Meet the Instruments" or "Introduction to the Orchestra" are two titles.

The music teacher in the school may assist with this activity, or the teacher designing the activity may choose his own examples from standard orchestral repertoire.

For example, the viola is well displayed in "Harold in Italy," by Berlioz; the flute in "Afternoon of a Faun" by Debussy; the piccolo in the *Chinese Dance* from the "Nutcracker Suite" by Tchaikovsky; the cello in *The Swan* from the "Carnival of Animals" by Saint-Saens.

Unexpected Outcomes

Once the listening station was set up with the tapes, the activity was not nearly as complicated as it might seem reading about it.

Mix and Match

Materials

Swatches of different types of materials
Colored construction paper (assorted colors)
Felt-tip pens
5 x 8 cards
Primary typewriter
Sheets of paper for list of terms and directions
Primary typewriter

Procedures

Check encyclopedia article on fabrics (or other reference) and choose from the types of fabrics listed distinctive items for which swatches can be provided.
Acquire swatches and mount them on construction paper.
Type one card for each swatch describing or defining distinctive characteristics of the material, but do not name the fabric.
Number the cards.
Post cards and swatches on bulletin board.
Post a list of names of fabrics represented by swatches. Make sure the numbers on the cards and the list arrangement are different.
Create caption and post it.
Create direction sheet and post it.
If other references than encyclopedias are to be used, place these on Reserve Shelf.

Student Behaviors

Student will number a sheet of paper to correspond with swatch numbers.
Student will use encyclopedia, or other references, to aid in matching fabric name with descriptive card definition.
Student will write the name of the fabric beside the swatch number.
Student will have answers checked.

Specific Examples

Wool Fiber or animal hair matted together by steam and
    pressure. (Felt)
Fabric with raised ribs running lengthwise. (Corduroy)
Cotton fabric woven with loops on the surface.   (Terry cloth)
Coarse, heavy cloth woven with yarns made from fibers of the
    jute plant. (Burlap)
A cloth with deep pile, usually two pieces woven at the same
    time. (Velvet)
Addition terms could include cotton, silk, wool, linen, leather,
    nylon, etc. or weaves such as chiffon, denim, satin,
    gingham, dotted Swiss, lace, etc.

Unexpected Outcomes

This format could be applied to identification of patterns
    such as paisley, herringbone, plaid, tattersall, calico,
    etc.
The various Scots tartan patterns could also be used.

Whosiwhatsits and Thingamabobs

Materials

Camera
Film
Construction paper
Felt-tip pens
Sheet of paper for directions

Procedures

Take a series of pictures of items found in or around the
    school building.
Make some of the pictures close-ups, showing only portions
    of the whole, and some of the pictures of obvious as well
    as obscure items.
Mount finished pictures on construction paper and number
    them.
Create caption and post it.
Create direction sheet and post it.

Student Behaviors

Student will number a piece of paper to match the pictured
    items and will write in identifications and locations of the
    pictured objects.
Student will have his answers checked when he has com-
    pleted the activity.

Specific Examples

Objects pictured could include the following:

Front door	Bathroom floor tile
Stage curtain pulley ropes	Basketball hoop

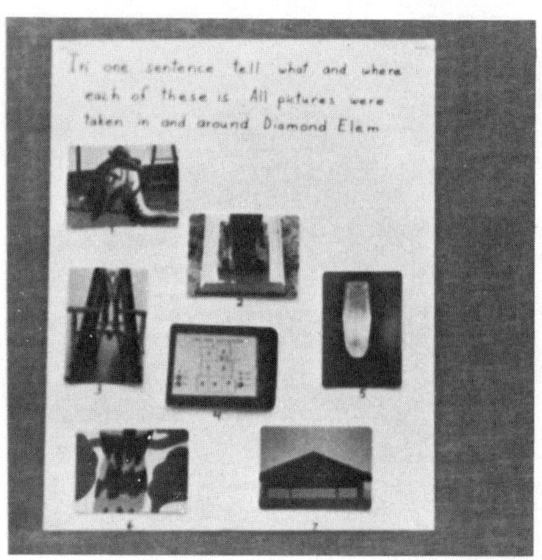

TV camera
Polywog (sit-upon)
Nurse's scale
Milk cartons
Office intercom buttons
Teachers' mailboxes
Custodian's dolly
Downspout
Carpet

Principal's auto or parking
   space
Softball backstop or home plate
Room number sign
Animal head erasers on media
   center pencils
Picture hanging in the hall
Plant on secretary's desk
Card catalog drawer pulls

Unexpected Outcomes

This activity lends itself well to help acquaint students with a new building.

Objects selected can be of items found in the surrounding community and include distinctive fences, walls, doorways, windows, roofs, etc.

Jump Rope Jingles

Materials

Use *Jump Rope!* by Peter L. Skolnik for rhymes (Workman
    Publishing Co., New York, 1974)
Primary typewriter
Sheets of typing paper
White construction paper
Colored felt-tip pens
Large-sized lettering stencils
Pictures of people or sketches of animals jumping rope

Procedures

Type individual jingles on sheets of typing paper with primary
    typewriter.
Post on bulletin board interspersed with pictures or sketches.
Create the caption and post it.
Create direction sheet and post it. (Directions urged stu-
    dents to learn as many new jingles as they could to use
    by themselves or on the playground.)

Student Behaviors

Student reads posted jingles and learns them.

Specific Examples

Classic rhyme

Teddy Bear, Teddy Bear, turn around
Teddy Bear, Teddy Bear, touch the ground
Teddy Bear, Teddy Bear, shine your shoe
Teddy Bear, Teddy Bear, that will do.

Teddy Bear, Teddy Bear, go upstairs
Teddy Bear, Teddy Bear, say your prayers
Teddy Bear, Teddy Bear, turn out the lights
Teddy Bear, Teddy Bear, say good night.

Counting rhyme

I had a little duck,
His name was Tiny Tim.
I put him in the bathtub
To see if he could swim.
He drank up all the water,
He ate up all the soap;
He died last night
With a bubble in his throat.
How many flowers did he have?
One, two, three. . . . . . .

Push rhyme

Down the Mississippi
Where the steamboats push . . .
(Second jumper pushes the first one out)

California oranges,
Tap me on the back.

Bump rhyme

(Jumper must let the top pass under the feet twice on one jump for
    italicized words)

Chewing gum, chewing gum,
Penny per *packet*.
First you chew it,
Then you *crack it*.
Then you stick it,
In your *jacket*.
Then you mother
Kicks up a *racket*.
Chewing gum, chewing gum,
Penny per *packet*.

Unexpected Outcomes

One second grade class used this activity to create their part
    in the annual all-school program. They chose rhymes
    from the four basic categories.
Many physical education programs include jumping rope as
    one activity. This provides a suitable time for cooperation
    with that department.

Name the Game:
Sports

Materials

Pictures of a variety of athletic competitions taken from
    magazines, newspapers, or the picture file
Construction paper
5 x 8 cards
Primary typewriter

Procedures

Mount each picture on construction paper.

Cut index cards in half and type a number on each half card
to place beside the pictures for identification purposes.

Arrange the board in two sections. The first contains pictures of more familiar sports; the second contains those
of less familiar sports.

Cut letters for the caption and post it.

Prepare a direction sheet and post it.

Student Behaviors

Students numbered their answer papers to match the numbers identifying pictures.

Younger students were asked to complete the first section
only while the upper grade students were asked to complete both sections.

Students wrote the names of the sports after the numbers.

Specific Examples

The following groupings were used:

Part 1:

1. Baseball
2. Basketball
3. Football
4. Tennis
5. Ping pong
6. Boxing
7. Ice hockey
8. Horse racing
9. Swimming
10. Golf
11. Diving
12. Auto racing
13. Figure skating
14. Ski jumping
15. Sailing

Part 2:

1. Track
2. Rugby
3. Fencing
4. Crew races
5. Lacrosse
7. Handball
7. Gymnastics
8. Bobsled racing
9. Archery
10. Wrestling
11. Pole vaulting
12. Jousting (State sport of Maryland)
13. Soccer
14. Field hockey
15. Sky diving

Unexpected Outcomes

Sports is a topic that motivates even the youngest students. First grade students, for whom writing the answers was a great frustration, were allowed to give their answers verbally to media center personnel.

Floor Plan
Orientation Exercise

Materials

Ditto master and paper for duplicating floorplans
Ruler
Ball point pen
Felt-tip pen
Construction paper (2 pieces)
List of areas and materials housed in media center
Directions for doing the project

Procedures

Construct a floor plan of the media center on a ditto master
and duplicate copies so that each student has his own.
Include shelving, tables, storage, carrels, work areas, and any
special equipment locations such as pencil sharpeners or
book return drop.
On one piece of construction paper list alphabetically items
to be located in the media center and noted on the floorplan answer sheet.
On the other sheet of construction paper print the directions
for the project.

Student Behaviors

Student reads items on the list and locates them in the media
center and then notes them on the floorplan.
The student should become acquainted with both the services
and the lay-out of the media center through this project.

Specific Examples

Locate: Reference section, Fiction, Non-fiction, Magazines, Easy and Picture Books, Biography, Film strips, Tapes, Kits, Phonorecords, Display Case(s), Workroom, Carrels, Previewers, Listening Stations, Fire Exits, Circulation Desk, Book Return Drop, Wastebaskets, and Pencil Sharpeners.

Unexpected Outcomes

Some students had not mastered map reading and had problems retaining proper room/floorplan orientation. The number of items on the list can be adjusted to the needs of the age level.

Table of Contents Game

Materials

3 x 5 cards
Standard size typewriter
Laminating supplies and equipment
Selection of books with tables of contents

Procedures

Place books on Reserve Shelf.
Work backwards from the answer, through the table of contents, to devise a question suitable for each book on the Reserve Shelf.

Type the question on one side of the card, and type the
author, title, and call number on the other side.
Laminate both sides of the cards.
Place the question card inside the cover of the book to be
used. (For more advanced students the cards can be
kept in a pack and the student can do the matching of
card and book.)

Student Behaviors

The student selects a book from the Reserve Shelf.
The student reads the question and attempts to locate the
chapter containing the answer to the question by means
of the table of contents. (It is advisable to have the
answer appear in the first few paragraphs or be associated with an illustration so that it is easily found.)
Student can give answers verbally or in written form, depending upon the size of the group playing the game.

Specific Examples

Sample questions:
1. How long does a hair live? *Anatomy* by Goldsmith 612
2. If you are making salt clay, and it is sticky, what do you
   need to add to make it stop sticking? *Let's Be
   Early Settlers With Daniel Boone* by Parrish 745.5
3. Which chapter has the largest number of pages?
   Volcanoes by Lauber 551.2
4. A cord of wood makes what size stack? *Logging* by
   Taylor 634.9
5. If you are making Capt. Hook's Poison Cake, at what
   temperature should you set the oven? *Storybook
   Cookbook* by MacGregor 641.5

Unexpected Outcomes

Students did not want to stop when the time was up.

Basic Reference Book
Search Questions

Materials

The books in reference section of the media center
3 x 5 cards
Felt pen, or
Primary typewriter

Procedures

Decide which ten reference books are to be studied.
Create ten questions especially appropriate for each title.
Identify all ten questions from a single reference with the same number. (There will be ten 1's, ten 2's, etc.)
Group questions in packs of ten cards, one question from each title. (Pack now contains cards numbered 1 through 10).
Next, label all cards in one pack of ten with a letter. (1-A; 2-A; 3-A; etc. 1-B; 2-B; etc.)
Each participating student will have his own pack of question cards.
Instruct each student to work through the questions in sequence, and assign each student a different number to begin with. This system reduces bunching and waiting to use references.

Student Behaviors

Each student begins with his assigned beginning question and works until he has answered all ten questions, writing the answers on notebook paper.
(This activity needs continuous assistance if it is to be successful. Someone must be scheduled to assist students. Otherwise they tend to become easily frustrated the first time through an exercise of this type.)

Specific Examples

1. *Atlas*
   Find a map showing the location of ______. (City, state)
   Give book title and page number.

2. *Almanac*
   Who won the Pulitzer Prize for music in ______? (Year)
   Give composer's name and title of his winning compo-
   sition.

3. *Geographic or Social Studies Series*
   Which encyclopedia has more information about ______?
   (Country)
   Give book title and page numbers.

4. *Science encyclopedia*
   Find a diagram of a ______. (Take a question from each
   volume)
   Give book title, volume, and page.

5. *Poetry index*
   Find a poem about ______. (Subject)
   Give poem title, code letters, and complete title of an-
   thology containing poem.

6. *Biographical dictionary*
   What was ______'s occupation? (use different people's
   names)
   Give occupation, book title, and page.

7. *Mathematics dictionary*
   What does *geodesic* mean? (Use different terms)
   Give meaning, book title, page.

8. *Author encyclopedia*
   List the names of two books written by ______ (Use different authors)

9. *Famous First Facts*
   Look up your birthday in the "Day" section, and find
   something that happened on that day.

   Note the year this event occurred. Next, find that year in
   the "Year" section, and choose an additional event
   that interests you.

Write down your birthday (month and day), and the two
events you chose.

10. *Quotation book*
Find a quotation about ______. (Subject)
Who said it? Give page number where the answer is
found.

Famous Firsts
(for the First Month)

Materials

The book, *Famous First Facts*, published by Wilson
Primary typewriter
5 x 8 cards
Construction paper in assorted colors
Felt-tip pens
Sheet of paper for directions

Procedures

Read through the January section of *Famous First Facts*
    selecting "firsts" which should appeal to students.
Type a description of each event used, one per card, and
    number the cards.
Using construction paper, and felt-tip pens, create some il-
    lustrations for the events.
Arrange cards and illustrations on the bulletin boards.
Put *Famous First Facts* on the Reserve Shelf.
Create caption and post it.
Create direction sheet and post it.

Student Behaviors

Student will number a piece of paper to match the number of
    items on the board.
Student will use *Famous First Facts* to find out the precise
    date of each happening.
Student will write that date beside the corresponding number
    of his answer sheet.
Student will have his answer checked.

Specific Examples

Gold discovered in California (January 24, 1848)
Typewriter ribbon (January 24, 1888)

X-ray photograph (January 12, 1896)
Patent for canning in tins (January 19, 1825)
Electric watch (January 3, 1957)
Drinking straw (January, 1888)
Ice cream cone rolling machine (January 29, 1924)
Color TV broadcast (January 1, 1954)
Auto race track (January 30, 1910)

Unexpected Outcomes

Student began to check other dates, such as their birthdates,
and then began to use other indexes within *Famous
First Facts*.

Decorate Your Door
as a Book Jacket

Materials

Roll bulletin board paper in assorted colors
Construction paper in assorted colors
Felt pens in assorted colors
Opaque projector
Classroom door (Difficult in an open school, but ends of cubby holes or book cases may be used to provide each participating group something standard in size).
Class's choice of favorite book

Procedures

Have each class choose the book for which they will create a "door jacket."
Cover the door with bulletin board paper.
Using any medium desired, have the students create component parts for the "door jacket."
The final design must include author, title, and some student art work.
When all displays are completed, set up a schedule allowing all classes to view all the displays.

Student Behaviors

As a classroom group, they choose the book title and join in creating the display.

Specific Examples

A second grade classroom chose *Millions of Cats*. Each student drew, colored, and cut out a cat.

A fourth grade classroom chose *Charlotte's Web*. They made a three-dimensional string web with a spider attached.

The cafeteria door bore *The Giant Sandwich* by Agnew.

The health room door had the illustration from *Burt Dow, Deepwater Man* in which a bandaid is placed upon a whale's tail.

The language resource room door was *The Case of the Bare Door* which they awarded the Noberry Award for the "least outstanding contribution to children's literature."

Since the language resource room was not a classroom unit, the teacher made the best of a bare door. The criteria for selecting prize books were discussed as part of her program.

Unexpected Outcomes

Classrooms usually have a single door. The media center had three doors!

Puzzles to be Worked
on Chalkboards

Materials

Reclaimed X-ray film or other transparency film
Opaque copy of the puzzle for creating transparency with
    machinery or by hand
Overhead projector
Chalkboard, chalk and eraser

Procedures

Create puzzle or copy one from a commercial source. These
    are often constructed around a seasonal or holiday
    theme.
Make the transparency.
Project it onto chalk board.
The answers are written directly on the chalkboard.

Student Behaviors

This activity lends itself to individual, small group, or class-
    room group participation.
The student participates according to the style dictated by the
    size of the participating group.

Specific Examples

Puzzle types may be hidden pictures, hidden words, cross-
    words, crossword, rhyming words, numbers, dot-to-dot,
    etc.
Good sources for prepared puzzles are books of puzzles,
    childrens' magazines, and childrens' pages in news-
    papers.

Unexpected Outcomes

If the student likes the puzzle idea he will work puzzles the year
    round regardless of the puzzle theme.
A need for a careful filing system develops. Organization by
    monthly folders works well.

Balloon Board

Materials

An assortment of small-sized inexpensive balloons
Some object to attach balloons to
List of questions for students to answer
Slips of paper to type questions on
Primary typewriter

Procedures

Write questions on slips of paper and place one slip inside
    each balloon.
Inflate the balloon and knot or otherwise seal the end.
Attach balloons to the object or hang them.

Student Behaviors

Student selects a balloon, pops it, reads the question, and
    tries to answer it.

Specific Examples

Questions may be from any content area.
Preparation for the game increases student reading.
Reading can be directed to the general collection for a topic
or to a Reserve Shelf.

Unexpected Outcomes

This method of chance selection can be used for choosing
report topics.

Color Word Recognition
(First Grade Project)

Materials

A large piece of white paper (One for each first grade class
participating)
A line drawing containing many small sections in the design
Black felt-tip pen
Opaque projector

Procedures

Draw freehand or enlarge with the opaque projector the design on the white paper.
Label each section of the drawings with one of the color
words.
Use a black felt-tip pen for both the outline and the color
words.

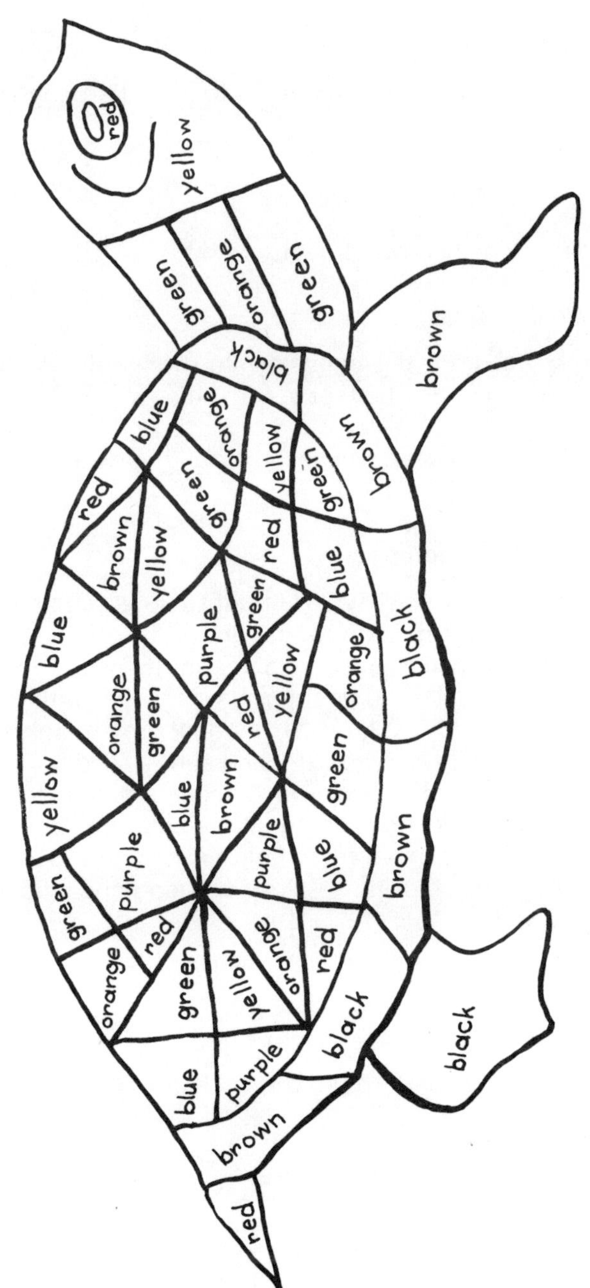

red
yellow
green
green
orange
blue
black
brown
blue
red
orange
orange
yellow
green
brown
green
yellow
red
green
blue
brown
blue
green
purple
yellow
orange
black
orange
green
red
purple
brown
green
yellow
blue
brown
green
purple
red
brown
green
yellow
purple
red
yellow
blue
orange
red
green
black
black
blue
purple
brown
red

Student Behaviors

Part of the first grade curriculum is to learn to recognize color
 words and colors.
When students have gained this skill in the classroom, the
 teacher sends them to color in "their" sections of the
 design.
Student brings his own crayons with him.

Specific Examples

Most activities are designed for students with greater skills
 than beginning first graders. This project is for them
 alone.
A turtle is a good design to use. If more than one is used, label
 with teacher's name.

Unexpected Outcomes

Many upper grade students thought it was unfair that they
 could not participate in this activity!
It took much longer than anticipated for the shells to be completed since the original turtle was drawn with too many
 sections. Four sections per student are enough.
The sketch included herewith has been revised.
Cooperation with the classroom teacher is needed to keep the
 "fast finishers" from doing all the coloring. One possible
 solution is to have the whole class come to the media
 center for a coloring session. Non-coloring students may
 browse.

Thematic Historical
Fiction Book Report

Materials

Fiction books with a historical setting (Any country or period
of time could be used to supply the theme)
Set of directions

Procedures

Select books with appropriate settings and reading levels.
There should be a few more books than students to
allow everyone some degree of choice.
Create direction sheet which consists of a set of questions
to be answered as part of each student's written book
report.

Student Behaviors

Student reads his chosen book, determining time and place of
   the setting.
Student then researches this period in history and geographic
   area in order to answer the questions.
The written book report is turned in to the classroom teacher.

Specific Examples

The set of questions used was as follows:
   1. When and where did the story take place?
   2. What was happening in the United States at that
       time?
   3. What was happening in the rest of the world at that time?
   4. Who was a famous person living at that time?

Unexpected Outcomes

The idea of every student using the same theme for a book
   report caught on.
Other themes might include the following:
   1. Biography
   2. Personification (*Little Toot, Mike Mulligan And His
       Steam Shovel, Miss Osborne, the Mop*)
   3. Fantasy (*Charlotte's Web, Genie of Sutton Place,
       Phantom Toll Booth*)
   4. Factual animal
   5. Folktale
   6. Poem (Each student chose his own short poem,
       memorized it, and recited it to the class)
   7. Factual countries
   8. States—Factual or fictional
   9. Rivers

Book Jacket Puzzles

Materials

Shirt cardboards, posterboard, etc. Felt-tip pens
Bookjackets Pressure sensitive labels
Laminating supplies and
    Dry-mount press
Boxes to store puzzles in
Paper cutter

Procedures

Select section of bookjacket to be mounted and trim off excess.

Mount bookjacket on cardboard.

Laminate top side only.

Cut with paper cutter into geometric shapes. Jackets of picture and easy books should be cut into fewer pieces than those for more advanced readers.

Each piece of a particular puzzle should be labeled with a distinctive code to facilitate returning separated pieces to proper storage box. These codes can be written on the reverse side of pieces with a felt-tip pen.

On the storage box, put a label stating the name of the book, the code that appears on the reverse side of the puzzle pieces, and the number of pieces in the completed puzzle. The latter number should be included for two reasons: 1) It quickly establishes level of difficulty, and 2) the puzzle can be checked quickly for completeness without being reassembled.

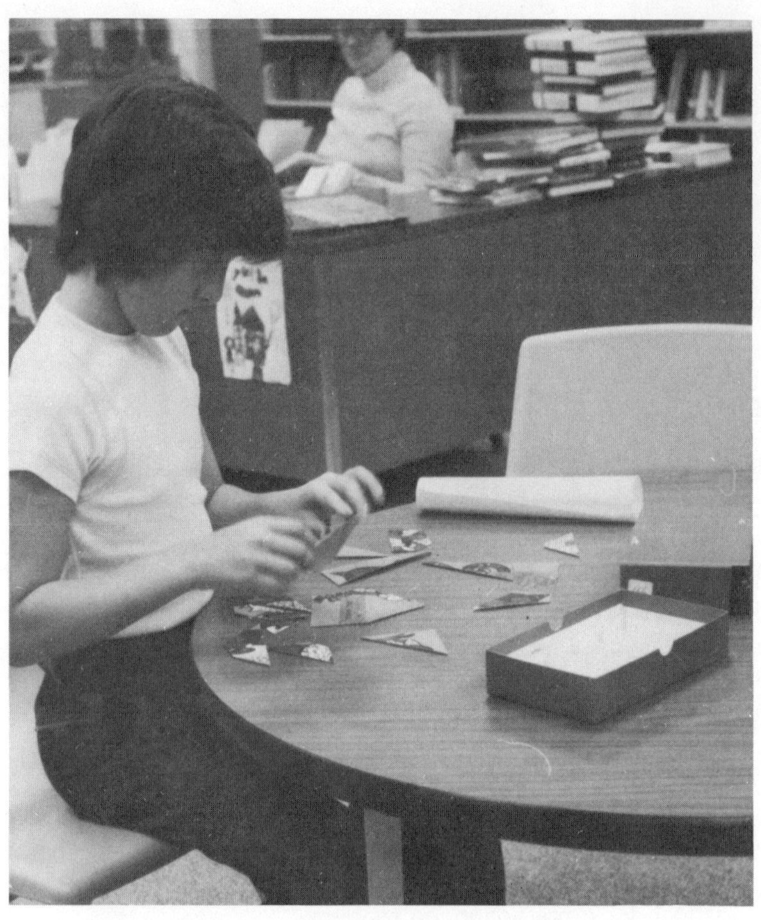

Student Behaviors

Students select a puzzle and put it together.
Sometimes they have already read the book, but frequently
doing the puzzle leads them to reading the book.

Unexpected Behaviors

Because there are no interlocking elements in the puzzle
pieces, it is easier to work the puzzle on a non-slippery
surface.

Flopovers: Sequence Puzzles

Materials

Cardboard
Cloth tape
Tearsheet pictures (from magazines, coloring books)
Mounting and laminating supplies
Dry-mount press
Felt-tip pens
Paper cutter
Storage containers for puzzle pieces
Sheet of paper for directions

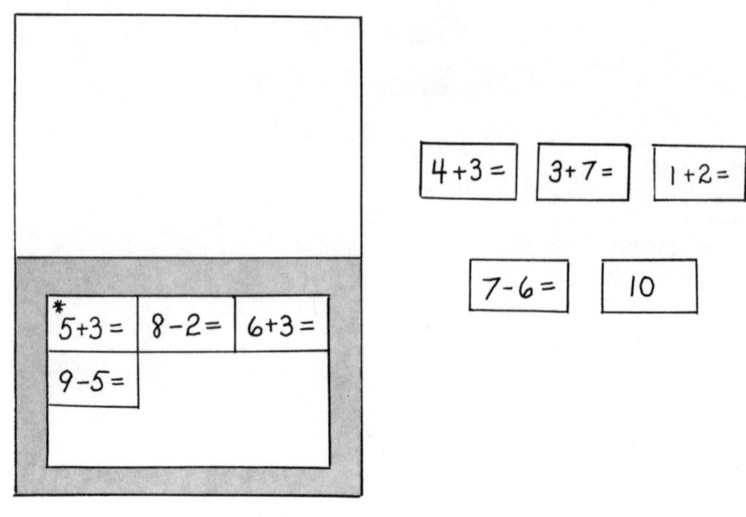

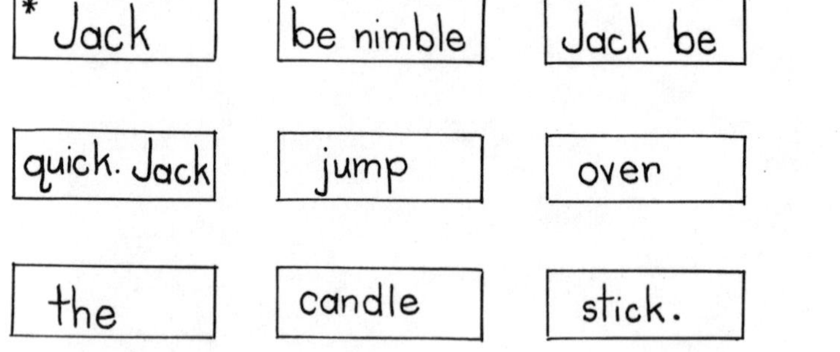

Procedures

Construct the Flopover frame.

Cut two pieces of cardboard each 12" x 14"

Cut 2" strips of cardboard, two of them 14" long and two of
them 8" long

Using cloth tape, fasten the 2" strips at the perimeter, but on
top of the large piece of cardboard

This creates an 8" x 12" opening within the "pictureframe."
(It is within this space that the student works the puzzle.)

Using cloth tape, hinge the second large piece of card-
    board to the frame along *one* side only.
Set the completed Flopover aside.
To create the puzzles, mount the tearsheet picture on a piece of
    cardboard, 6¾" x 11¾".
On the reverse side, lightly draw lines to form rectangles of
    equal size which will be used as cutting guides.
On the reverse side, write the message using a felt-tip pen.
Space the message so that it flows sequentially left to right
    and top to bottom.
Make sure there are no identical pieces of message on
    rectangles.
Mark the upper left hand corner of the first rectangle with an
    asterisk to indicate the start of the puzzle.
The puzzle pieces are fitted into the "picture frame" opening
    with the message side up and properly sequenced.
The hinged cover is closed and held tightly while the entire
    Flopover is inverted.
If the sequencing of the message has been accurate, the pic-
    ture viewed when the Flopover cover is raised should be

correct. Be sure to test a puzzle before giving it to students to work.

Store a direction sheet with each puzzle. Several puzzle fillers can be stored separately in envelopes and used with a single Flopover frame.

Specific Examples

Language and mathematical skills are equally adaptable to this format. See diagram.

Unexpected Outcomes

There needs to be a fairly close tolerance in size between puzzle sheet and Flopover "picture frame" opening to prevent sliding of pieces during inversion.

If standard sizes are used, only as many frames are needed as students working puzzles at the same time require.

Student Created
Book Marks

Materials

Newsprint or other scrap paper cut into 2" x 8½" strips
Ditto masters
Duplicating machine
Duplicating paper
Paper cutter

Procedures

Have students draw with pen or pencil a design on scrap
  paper strip. The student must follow the directions con-
  cerning content and size. The student's name and classroom identification must be included.
These designs are then traced onto ditto masters by the
  media staff and copies are run off.
Using the 2" x 8½" dimensions, five designs can be made
  from a single master.
After designs are run off, they are cut apart for distribution.

Student Behaviors

Student designs a bookmark based on the current theme or
  books included in the specific directions.

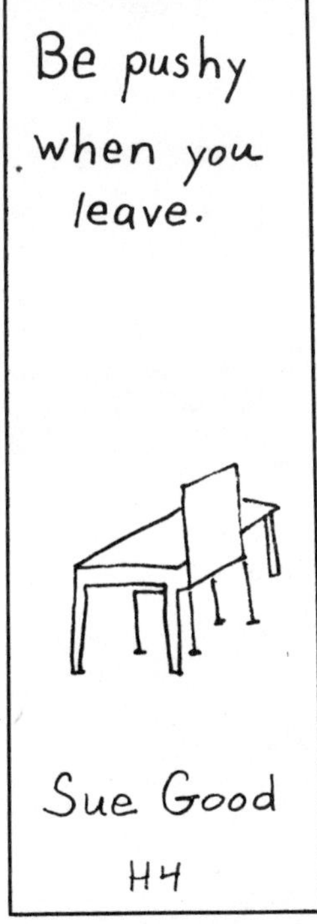

Specific Examples

Possible themes include the following:
1. Holiday motifs. (Don't overlook special weeks such as National Library Week, Brotherhood Week, Dental Health Week, etc. in addition to the traditional holidays.)
2. Favorite books. (Designs should include author, title, and a distinctive illustration.)
3. Media center courtesy or assistance.

Unexpected Outcomes

Using the designer's name on the bookmark credits the student's work, but it also influences selection for use by fellow students. Those bookmarks designed by popular students are taken first, regardless of the cleverness of the design.

Judicious selection of designs by the media staff can provide a source of attention for a child who is often overlooked.

Appendixes

Overlapping Applications

Activities are listed under subject in section II. A number of these activities could prove useful in more than one category. They are listed below, followed by the additional subject areas that might be considered.

Student Skill Development

Involvement activities are designed to provide learning opportunities for students. The following list identifies skills which can be fostered by the activity named.

Study Skills:
1. Classifying
    Borrowed Words, page 97
    National Wildlife Week "Net a Pet," page 32
    Vegetable Soup, page 87

2. Encyclopedias—Using the index
    Bicentennial Celebration No. 2, page 71
    National Wildlife Week "Net a Pet," page 32

3. Encyclopedias—Using sub-headings
    Christmas Traditions Around the World, page 20
    Circus Information, page 28
    Do You "Snow" the Answer? page 24
    Kite Flying, page 30

4. Following Directions
    All projects

5. Map Skills
    Floorplan Orientation, page 110
    North, South, East, West Overhead Projector
        Game, page 77
    Read Your Way Across the USA, page 62
    Winnie the Pooh, page 43

10. Telling Time
    Timely Questions, page 92

11. Vocabulary Building
    Borrowed Words, page 97
    Color Word Recognition, page 122
    Find the Animal Word, page 26
    National Wildlife Week "Net a Pet," page 32
    Puzzles Worked on Chalkboard, page 120
    Seasonal Dictionary Game, page 19
    Word and Phrase Origins, page 66

12. Writing
    Bicentennial Celebration II, page 71
    Historical Fiction Thematic Book Report, page 125
    Kite Poems, page 48
    Word and Phrase Origins, page 66

Reading Complete Books:

Some of the activities require the reading of complete books. They are the following:

1. Animal of the Month, page 55
2. Author/Title Crossword Puzzle, page 57
3. Beatrix Potter, page 38
4. Bulletin Board Bingo, page 60
5. Decorate Your Door as a Book Jacket, page 118
6. Historical Fiction Thematic Book Report, page 125
7. Read Your Way Across the USA, page 62
8. What Story Do I Live In? page 53
9. Winnie the Pooh, page 43

Puzzles:

Much can be learned through the playing of games. Puzzles of all types are valuable in this respect. Activities based on the use of puzzles include the following:

1. Author/Title Crossword Puzzle, page 57
2. Beatrix Potter (Crossword Puzzle), page 38

Bibliography

The following books are typical of those available to assist the instructor with the problems of lettering, laminating, layout, collection of materials, and the use of machinery.

Brown, James W., ed.
An AV Instructional Technology Manual for Independent Study, 4th ed.
New York: McGraw-Hill Book Company, 1973.

Erickson, Carlton W. H. and Curl, David H.
Fundamentals of Teaching with Audiovisual Technology.
New York: Macmillan Company, 1972.

Hill, Donna
The Picture File; A Manual and Curriculum Related Subject Heading List.
Hamden, Ct.: Shoe String Press, 1975
(Also available in paper from Gaylord Bros., Inc., Syracuse, N.Y. 13201)

Garvey, Mona
Teaching Displays, Their Purpose, Construction, and Use.
Hamden, Ct.: Shoe String Press, 1972

Kemp, Herrold E.
Planning and Producing Audiovisual Materials, 3rd ed.
New York: Thomas Y. Crowell, 1975.

Richardson, Wilmont H.
Freehand Lettering.
New York: Sterling Publishing Company, 1960.

Schultz, Morton J.
*The Teacher and Overhead Projector: A Treasury of Ideas,
    Uses, and Techniques.*
Englewood Cliffs, New Jersey: Prentice-Hall, Inc., 1965.

Wankelman, Willard F., et al.
Handbook of Arts and Crafts, 3rd ed.
Dubuque, Iowa: Wm. C. Brown Company Publishers, 1974.